WATERING THE DESERT

For Pat,
who will be missed forever

Watering the Desert

with Tony de Mello

John Callanan, SJ

Mercier Press

Mercier Press receives financial assistance from
the Arts Council/An Chomhairle Ealaíon

First published in 2004 by Mercier Press
Douglas Village, Cork
Website: www.mercierpress.ie

Trade enquiries to CMD Distribution
55A Spruce Avenue, Stillorgan Industrial
Park, Blackrock, County Dublin
Tel: (01) 294 2560; Fax: (01) 294 2564
E-mail: cmd@columba.ie

© John Callanan, 2004
ISBN 1 85635 444 X
10 9 8 7 6 5 4 3 2 1

A CIP record for this title is available
from the British Library

Printed in Ireland by ColourBooks,
Baldoyle Industrial Estate, Dublin 13

CONTENTS

FOREWORD

Usually, the introductory comments of a book like this let you know what the subject matter inside is going to be like. I think it's only fair, however, to let you know also what these pages do not contain. If you are looking for a historical biography of Anthony de Mello you won't find it here. Similarly, if you seek an extensive overview of his philosophy of life, you are likely to be disappointed.

So what does the book hope to do? It starts by trying to respond to the questions that I most often find myself answering about the type of prayer Anthony de Mello fostered and encouraged. It attempts to highlight the kinds of problems a person might encounter when they engage in the praying process. It also gives a taste of the sort of benefits you might reap if you devote time and energy to the type of prayer Anthony de Mello promulgated. I hope also that it may revitalise you in your exploration of different prayer styles and help you in your own individual journey towards God.

At the end of each chapter I present a number of prayer exercises and meditations that you may find helpful. If you attempt one each day, you will not only get into the habit of meditation fairly quickly but you will also see whether you find the practice profitable or not for you.

Finally, very many thanks to Eddie O'Donnell, SJ, and to Colm Wynne for checking the manuscript and to my brother, Bill, for his illustrations.

John Callanan, SJ
Dublin, March 2004

INTRODUCTION

Since my first book on Anthony de Mello was published, much has happened in the Roman Catholic Church. Not all of it has been good. Many of those who are active in Church affairs and supportive to religious life in general have felt mortified by recent events that have taken place in ecclesiastical circles. I believe that – at least in Ireland – these feelings of shame may have occurred because of the constant stream of bad publicity, scandals and abuses that have been highlighted in the media on a regular basis. While this goes on, the gift that Anthony de Mello was and is to the Church has gone through interesting developments. On the one hand, those who valued what he had to say continue to use his insights. In fact, they have almost sanctified his memory. At much the same time, some elements within the ecclesiastical hierarchy have moved in the opposite direction. It seems they have become more and more worried by the sense of inner freedom that the thinking and teaching of de Mello appear to inspire among his followers. They hint that it may be injurious to your spiritual health if you read his material or follow his prayer style.

So first we have to ask and answer some questions about the man and his work. Who was Anthony de Mello? Where did he come from? How did he develop a prayer style that has helped so many? Is he safe? Why did some in the Vatican choose to speak out against him? Finally, are we likely to find what he teaches helpful?

Anthony de Mello was born on 4 September 1931, in Bombay, India. I think it would not be overstating the case if I said that he had a profound influence on all those who came into contact with him. Early biographical details are scarce and difficult enough to come by, but he himself has said that some of his initial faith enthusiasm was most probably given to him during his earliest childhood Indian experiences.

A friend who knew him in his youth tells me that he was always sharp and bright. To illustrate this, that same friend speaks about an incident from de Mello's youth that had far-reaching consequences for all concerned. One day, Anthony came home from school and announced that he wanted to become a Catholic priest. This went very much against Indian tradition for the eldest son in a family was usually expected to carry on the family name. His father spoke with him explaining that, as he was the only son at home, certain expectations rested on his shoulders. In essence, his presence was required to carry on the family traditions and name. This meant that Anthony's fondest wishes and dreams would have to be put on hold. It was at this point that fate stepped in to give him a helping hand.

The story goes that Anthony's mother remained childless for some years after Anthony's father made this pronouncement. Eventually, word seeped out that Anthony's mother was expecting again. As she was rushed to hospital so that her newborn child might be delivered, Anthony is reported to have run the four miles or so to the hospital to find out whether the baby was a boy or a girl. On hearing the news that he had a new brother, he is reported to have said to his father, 'Great, now I can become a priest'.

Whatever about the truth of this story, it's safe to say that during his early years de Mello – though a Christian – was exposed to both Hindu and Buddhist traditions. He joined the Society of Jesus straight after school and began his basic formation as a Jesuit in Bombay. After an initial two years in the Jesuit noviceship, he was sent abroad for a variety of studies. He took on the study of philosophy in Barcelona, psychology at Loyola University in Chicago, and theology at the Gregorian University in Rome. While in Europe, he was profoundly influenced by the works of a number of Spanish saints and Christian mystical writers – most notably Teresa of Avila and John of the Cross. Some observers have noted that the fusion of those three elements – the study of psychology in the United States, his own Indian background, and the reflections upon the theories of good and evil contained in both eastern and western spirituality – provided de Mello with insights which produced a heady cocktail.

His impact upon western spirituality happened slowly. In 1974, he was elected as a delegate from the Jesuit Province of Bombay to the General Congregation of the Society of Jesus in Rome. Each day, before the proceedings of the congregation began, many of the delegates prayed together and Anthony de Mello was asked to conduct these prayer sessions. For half an hour each day, in English and Spanish, he led the proceedings.

These conferences obviously left a deep impression on those who attended. We are told that his prayer groups began each day with a period of silence. This was followed by a short chant. De Mello suggested that the use of chants, the repetition of certain words (such as the name of Jesus), allied with measured breathing, self-awareness and a relaxed body position, would assist the participants to find their way to God. He stressed that God is already present in our lives. The participants' principle task was to become fully aware of that fact.

During his lifetime, it might be fair to say that Anthony de Mello was something of a 'guru', an inspiration, a beacon of hope and a fountain of wisdom to many. Most who had contact with him, either through his workshops on prayer, or even through his videos, maintain that he could hold master-classes in prayer like no one else. He was able to breathe gently on dying embers of faith and, when he did, sparks of new prayer life were ignited. These re-ignited fires were a boost for those whose spiritual life had become weak or tepid. A brief time in his presence meant that those grown faint-hearted were likely to be infected with his marvellous enthusiasm. Their life, as well as their faith, often received a shot in the arm.

More than ever today, that zest for vitality and life is much sought after. Equally, many seek gurus who have the unique ability to breathe life, verve and dynamism into those they encounter. De Mello had that gift and was such a mentor, capable of bringing sparkle and effervescence to those he met. His particular gift and relevance now may be that he dared to challenge – but challenge in a constructive manner. No one likes to be challenged, not even – or perhaps least of all – the institutional Church, but in our better moments both it and we can sometimes admit that such a challenge might be necessary. It may force us to both search for – and find – the living Christ within us.

This notion initially began to plant itself in my mind during Anthony de Mello's first visit to Ireland in 1977. I suspect most Jesuits in the country had never heard of this strange Indian before that date. His name began to appear on Jesuit radar screens after those energising prayer inputs with fellow Jesuits at the 32nd General Congregation of the Society of Jesus in Rome. Possibly because of these, he was invited to Ireland and asked to present a workshop on prayer for any Irish Jesuits who might wish to attend. About 60 did. I was among them. Almost as soon as he arrived, you could sense the electricity in the air. The way he spoke about prayer was riveting. His words and theories had a fresh feel about them. The ambience he managed to create on that first evening with us was anything but predictable. In one sense it was shocking – at least to me.

I had just finished my own initial two years in the Society of Jesus at the time but can still remember the tremendous excitement that his words engendered. I was rocked and challenged to my very core – but I

was not the only one. Much more experienced citizens than myself were
also rocking and rolling in the aisles. Many spent the entire evening –
and much of the week that followed – spellbound. Questions arose in
each one of us and these questions were at once both refreshing and
frightening. While some disagreed with what he had to say during his
workshop sessions, I think very few were unmoved. Looking back now I
can see that Anthony de Mello touched and radically altered the lives
of many who attended that first seminar – but how did he do that?

The question is partly answered by two short statements. Firstly,
those who took the time to be with him on workshops were touched not
only by what he taught, but also by the vitality with which he taught it.
Secondly, a lot of what he had to say was profound and also stimulating.
His message seemed to have lasting value. This fact was mentioned repeatedly by those who were lucky enough to personally have been present at his spirituality courses in India or at his workshops or retreats on
prayer and spirituality throughout the world. De Mello started these
courses with a vision. He was looking for fire – the fire of faith – and his
workshops were noteworthy because they put that fire back in the bellies
of those who were open and amenable. During those retreats and seminars his energy was amazing. It never flagged. He seemed to enjoy and
gain vim from what he taught. He left his listeners with dignity and hope,
free to walk forward on their faith journey in the ways they thought best
and make decisions and resolutions for themselves. It was fairly obvious
that he felt many were motoring through life on half throttle. They lack-
ed daring and courage. In a sense, they were asleep and it began to dawn
on many that if they could just take the first step forward in faith development, many more steps might follow. Various ghosts that had held
them back in the past, might, with considerable effort, be banished.

So the message at the workshops was sharp and serious, but, despite the gravity of the content, humour was always present. De Mello
had a sort of mantra for those who had ears to hear and courage to act:
'Don't just do something, sit there. Try to go deeper'. He would encourage this exploration by using a favourite phrase of his from the east:
'When a people stop travelling, they arrive'. He asked participants to
stop whatever they were doing, relax, become quiet, and attempt bravely
to come into the present. This, he promised, would heighten interior
awareness. Each individual was asked to become present to whatever
might be going on within them, shutting things neither out nor off, in
order to discover where God might be working in their lives.

Anthony de Mello was an explosive teacher and speaker when it came to looking at the whole area of spiritual development and growth. He had the rare gift of bestowing vitality and spiritual energy wherever he went. He encouraged silence, because he believed that inner stillness brings clarity. He wanted his audiences to discover the revelation that silence brings. He was keen on encouraging techniques for 'going beyond'. He didn't say this was easy. In fact, he didn't even say precisely what this meant. As a starter, he would advise participants at his workshops to undertake an experiment. He advised them to take up a posture they were comfortable with. They should then lightly close their eyes and maintain silence for a period of ten minutes or thereabouts. They might begin by soaking themselves in the stillness and just seeing what revelations this silence might bring to the surface. At the end of the ten minutes he often invited the participants to share with others what each had experienced and felt. Sometimes members found it helpful to jot down their insights on paper before they began to relate them verbally. This exercise moved swiftly, and most found it fun. Making it fun was part of Anthony de Mello's uniqueness.

The prayer practices he taught sprang from his own experience. By this I mean that if he had not found particular methods of prayer helpful in his own life, he neither encouraged nor recommended them to others. In fact he dropped them from his seminars.

I remember he told us once that he had been in charge of young clerical students after his own ordination and was expected to teach them good spiritual routines and practices. To this end, he did what any conscientious and reasonable individual might be expected to do and taught them as he had been taught himself. However, when his inexperienced charges began to question him about the most beneficial methods of prayer, he soon recognised that his exhortations and lessons were seriously deficient. What he was presenting was textbook material – but only that. His lectures were made up of supposed wisdom and techniques which he himself had been given by his elders, but were not in any way based on what he knew to be true from his own prayer practice. It slowly began to dawn on him that he wasn't practising what he was preaching. Perhaps more dishonestly, he wasn't preaching what he was practising. He thus began to formulate a very important principle for himself. He would test each prayer practice he spoke about before he put it before his students. He would take as his model the goldsmith.

The goldsmith, as de Mello explained it, tested all the materials he used by means of fire. He now determined to do the same. Henceforth he would see if the prayer practices he recommended would stand up to the day to day rigours of life. In that way he would be like the goldsmith – scraping, polishing and testing each scrap of material and each pearl of prayer wisdom to see if they proved to be true or false, wholesome or imperfect. By this method, he found that some of the spiritual advice he had previously offered was less effective than he might have supposed. In terms of the goldsmith, he realised that some of the materials he was using were base metal. From then on, he would only speak about prayer insofar as he had tried and tested the ideas for himself. If they proved to be beneficial and carried with them good fruit for the future, he included them on his agenda. Otherwise, they were dropped from his curriculum.

This method proved to be advantageous both for himself and his students. In time, his fame as a 'prayer guru' grew. He was sent to direct retreats at the 'Sadhana' Jesuit Prayer Centre near Bombay. Here, the basic simplicity and honesty of his approach proved immensely popular. His seminars and prayer workshops were much in demand. Each summer de Mello spent many weeks conducting workshops in Europe, North America, Australia, the Philippines and Japan. Packed crowds were the order of the day and those who attended were dazzled by his wit and wisdom. The philosophy and theology presented may have been wrapped in fable and story format and was beautifully delivered with a lightness of touch, but de Mello's listeners rarely missed the points that were being made. He seldom pulled his punches. He was hard-hitting and wonderfully lucid. Those who came with their heads in the clouds quickly brought themselves – or in some cases were brought – down to earth. They learned that most of us live mainly in our heads, which might not be the most sensible place to conduct our affairs. Up there, we tend to be less than awake or aware and thus are likely to miss the footprints that God leaves around us. We live too rarely in the now or in the present. Because of this, past mistakes and regrets are given more prominence than they deserve. Furthermore, we spend such vast quantities of time uselessly regretting what cannot be changed and crying over experiences that cannot be undone and so starve ourselves of opportunities for growth which may be staring us in the face. As well as that, we tend to project our minds forward and try to see into the future, wasting precious time and energy on events that might, or might not, ever come to pass. In this way we impair our own ability to grow. We allow ourselves be overwhelmed by feelings of dread about possible disasters which await us or we become disheartened by thoughts of challenges yet to be faced.

Participants on Anthony de Mello's workshops began to understand that he believed his task was to assist people to change themselves, not just their ideas. First they would have to work out what needed changing. After this, a second step forward would be necessary. A decision would have to be made and a question answered. Was the pain involved in effecting change possible and was it worth the effort? Were the individuals themselves prepared to put in the graft and spadework necessary for renewal? That's a painful question. It's even more distressing if the answer may well turn out to be negative.

As his workshop technique became more refined and sophisticated, de Mello conducted what were called 'Satellite' retreats in the United States and Canada. These were beamed by television to 76 universities around the North American continent. This meant that he could get his message out to 3,000 students at a time. He could also engage with them in face-to-face dialogue. His final retreat and the one that finally stilled his incessant enthusiasm for life, was held at Fordham University in New York during June 1987. In the course of that workshop his heart finally gave out. He had burnt his candle to the quick. His work and spirit, however, did not die with him.

In retrospect, we can see that Anthony de Mello touched and radically altered the lives of many. Even today, his name refuses to drop out of the headlines. Numerous books and retreats continue to draw on the inspiration he once provided. These workshops remain immensely popular and many find their prayer life greatly enhanced by attending them.

During his lifetime, Anthony de Mello was never very far from controversy. Perhaps it stimulated him. It continues to pursue him after his death. In the year 2000, the Congregation for the Faith in the Vatican put out a document, which might politely be likened to a 'Government Health Warning' about Anthony de Mello and his work. This caused a degree of sorrow and confusion for many. Those who admired the man and his teaching – and found it such an inspiration in their own lives – wondered why the document had been produced. Many still wonder and as far as I can find out, nothing further has been heard from Rome about the matter. It seems three issues worried the congregation. As I understand it, the documents asked first of all if de Mello mistakenly equated God with nature. Where they got this notion from I have some difficulty in understanding. In his videos, de Mello does speak of God and nature. He likens them to the dancer and the dance. He clearly states that they are not the same, but they are closely intertwined. Many people, it seemed to de Mello, caught glimpses of God in the beauty that surrounds them. They might be helped by imagining that the beauty of nature acts as a sort of mirror image and thus illustrates for us the beauty of God.

Secondly, the congregation, in its wisdom, seems to have difficulty with de Mello's views about God. Was Jesus God, or just another prophet? Where they got this idea from I have no way of knowing. Certainly if you look at his videos, or had heard him speak in person, it is hard to imagine how that impression could be formed. Those who watch and listen are normally struck by the great reverence which de Mello attaches to the second Person of the Trinity.

Finally, the congregation seemed to think that de Mello does not show, or have sufficient deference for, the institution of the Church. On these grounds I think de Mello might have pleaded guilty himself. Love of the Church is a great gift but if it is slavishly and uncritically followed it does neither the Church nor its followers any favours at all. If an institution is unable or unwilling to examine itself constructively from within, then its enemies will do so from without. In all probability, they will bring such an institution to its knees. Uncritical silence in such situations, I suspect, is not faithfulness, but unhelpful cowardice. Great love demands great honesty.

At the end of each chapter, you will find a number of breathing exercises, mediations and fantasy exercises. Try these out for yourself. A few very basic hints may help you.

Before you start out on an exercise, you should find yourself a comfortable space where you feel safe. It will help considerably if you are likely to be left undisturbed in this place for at least half an hour. You then read through the prayer exercise or meditation as I describe it and get down to work. Begin by building up an atmosphere of quiet and stillness so that there is at least the possibility that God can get to work.

Anthony de Mello mentioned that on many Indian retreats, the one conducting the prayer exercise begins by concentrating on an awareness of breath patterns. Some prayer masters hold that respiration acts as a bridge from the known to the unknown. In the quiet space that such practices provide, you notice that your mind wanders to and fro. It glides from events of the past towards dreams of the future and has difficulty – you might almost say an aversion – to staying in the present moment. Observing your breath helps you explore not only the reality of your body but also your mind. Material concealed in the unconscious rises to the conscious level and manifests itself in various physical or mental discomforts. It reveals something you may not have known – or more likely may not have wanted to admit – about yourself. If you occasionally find it difficult to sit still during such exercises, you may now know why. In order to help you get started, the following points may be helpful:

- Do not eat immediately before meditation as a full stomach is not conducive to calm and peace.
- Choose a relatively quiet room where you can be alone.
- You may well find that subdued lighting is helpful.
- A good posture, aided by a comfortable seat or prayer stool, will help.
- Try to avoid distractions and minimise obvious sources of disturbance such as noisy doorbells or phones. Take your phone off the hook, and meditate at a time when you can reasonably expect to be left alone.
- Do not finish your meditation too abruptly as your body is likely to be in a relaxed state as you taper towards a finish and emerging too suddenly leaves an unpleasant aftertaste.
- If, during meditation, you realise that your mind has drifted gently off the subject matter in hand, quietly bring it back to the area you are working on.
- Where possible, finish with an 'Our Father'.

*

EXERCISE ONE
An Exercise on Breath

As soon as you find a suitable spot for prayer, settle yourself down on a straight-backed chair and place your hands in your lap. Close your eyes and relax. Breathe in and out deeply and feel your whole upper body filling with air. Draw air in through your nostrils and imagine it entering your throat before coming down through your windpipe and towards your shoulder area. Allow it to then move slowly downwards through your arms and into your fingers. Imagine your chest area filling with air and notice that air then making its way – circling around your backbone – down to the pit of your stomach. If you place your hand over your belly button you should be able to feel it reaching the belly button spot. Now put a finger on your pulse and count the beats. Become aware of the rate. Use your pulse frequency as a guide and breathe in to the count of four. After a short pause, breathe gently out for a four- count. As you practise you may note your rate of breath intake has slowed down and this often produces a heightened, mind-calming effect. At first this may not be apparent, for any new activity takes time to master and meditation is no different – it takes a little preparation before you start.

Most of us have our minds bombarded with noise and confusion and thus a certain amount of winding down may be necessary before we begin. You need to relax and still the mind so, after you find a suitable place, try to become aware of how you feel at the moment. Are your mind and body reasonably still? Assume an upright position in a straight-backed chair and try to ensure that you are not slumped or bent over in your posture. Next close your eyes and see if you can become aware of the sensations that present themselves as your eyelids close. Notice the air as you breathe in and out. Just breathe normally and recognise the coolness of the air on each inward breath through your nose and the slightly warmer feel of it as you breathe out through your mouth. Keep up that quiet, gentle pattern of breathing in and out for a few minutes. Find out for yourself whether or not that practice brings tranquillity. When you feel suitably still and quiet, try the following exercise.

Imagine it is early morning and you are just waking up. The dawn is breaking and you can just see in your imagination the first rays of light streaking into the horizon. This is an early warning signal from the sun that it is about to rise and herald in a new day. Try to feel a sense of expectation for this is a new day coming to you from God that has never existed before. The day brings with it opportunities. It also carries new hopes, dreams and possibilities that you may be able to take advantage of. Pray that these new possibilities may not pass you by.

*

Exercise Two
An Attempt to be Grateful

Before you begin to pray, get your mind in order. Sit comfortably on a prayer stool or hard-backed chair in a quiet room. Make sure the room is one where you feel safe and where you will not be disturbed. Close your eyes and begin to become aware of your breathing. Don't change the depth or pace. Just direct your attention to your breath as it moves into your body through your nostrils and observe the sound and feel of the stale air as you exhale it. When you have begun to get a sense of your breath pattern, move on to an awareness of the feel of the air as it touches your skin. Notice its coolness as it begins its interior journey through your nostrils and experience the slightly different sensation as it makes its way out again through your mouth or nose some seconds later. As soon as you feel your body is somewhat relaxed, you can begin to orient your mind in a prayerful direction. Begin to think of one thing for which you are grateful. This might be your health, or your friends, or your job, or even your surroundings, or another good thing with which you have been blessed. When you have settled on one thing you are grateful for (let's suppose it is your sight), begin to realise that this very day many things have been opened up for you through the 'sight' channel. You may have been lucky enough to have passed through dazzling countryside, or been gifted with gorgeous weather. As you concentrate on the beauty of scenery or personality that have presented themselves to you, the realisation may begin to dawn that these things make you grateful just to be alive. Finish with the short prayer of the visionary, Juliana of Norwich, 'How lucky I am, how grateful I am.'

*

EXERCISE THREE
A Meditation on my Own Breath

Quieten yourself ...
Settle into a balanced comfortable position ...
Take a slow and deep breath ... count slowly up to four as you take each breath in and let each breath out.
Let out the breath with a deep sigh.
Continue with these deep and slow breaths for a couple of minutes ...
Just be quiet ... feel the calmness ... hear the silence ... sense the natural rhythm.
Concentrate on what is happening while you breathe: notice that the air is coldish coming in through your nostrils, warmer on its way out ...
Now relax completely and let your breath flow easily ... without effort. Just be aware of your natural breathing.
Whenever your mind wanders, take note of the wandering and return to an awareness of your breath pattern.
When you have spent some little time on this exercise, bring yourself back to the present place and time.

Searching for the Ox

The Ox-Herding Pictures: *Beginners in meditation often find their awareness wandering off at the least provocation. Unused to discipline, our mind appears to have an unruly will of its own which requires taming if we are to maintain our focus of attention for any length of time. These pictures, modelled on Zen Buddhist originals, form an allegory to illustrate this process. The final stage, represented by a blank circle, suggests a state of total self-absorption, where one has become oblivious of both one's mind operating and one's own unique identity.*

CHAPTER 1

GETTING STARTED

He prays best who does not know that he is praying
— St Anthony of Padua

Anthony de Mello was a master craftsman and an expert in matters of prayer. He wanted us to know – regardless of how we feel – that God always makes Himself available to us. Put simply, de Mello suggested that we can – if we so desire – instigate a conversation between God and ourselves. He did not claim that initiating and sustaining such a dialogue is easy. So is it? You may well imagine that answering the above question is straightforward. It should be easy enough to state clearly whether undertaking prayerful meditation is complicated or not. Anthony de Mello regularly spoke with a twinkle in his eye about how intelligible the ground-rules for prayer are. Occasionally he did mention how surprised he was that those who speak and write about the matter make it seem so intricate and complex. Sr Wendy Beckett, the English nun who writes so well on the subject, concurs. In one of her books she recalls how, in her early years, she met a bookish Jesuit who talked long and loud about the wisdom of finding time and space for God in our lives. During the course of his rather complicated ramblings he mentioned that the practice of talking to God was not too complex. 'I hope he truly believed that,' said the good sister, 'because his manner of delivery certainly didn't indicate that it was true'.

There are a number of common conceptions and misconceptions about prayer that may be worth looking at before we begin. For example, some ask whether meditation is a fix-all for every kind of problem? Can it right all ills, and can it do so quickly? 'No', is probably the most honest answer, though certainly prayer and meditation can bring renovation and change to our lives, even if all change is not necessarily good, and neither does it always indicate growth. Some people ask if they can expect the practice of meditation to be learned quickly and if it will be demanding – while others inquire as to whether they are likely to be bored and frustrated if they take it up? It seems only fair to tell them that many who write and speak about the nuts and bolts of prayer stress pain as well as gain. They say that as well as being invigorating and stimulating, it is hard, relentless and at times a bit of a grind.

To illustrate this, in India they like to talk about a guru who went to an ashram to teach the fundamentals of prayer. When he arrived, he found the room packed with students. The guru began by putting his finger to his lips and asking for complete silence. 'It's very noisy in here, please try to maintain silence', he beseeched. This amazed his onlookers. Many in the room felt the atmosphere to be serene and almost motionless. Only the anxious breathing of the students could be heard. Again the guru called out, 'Please, it is still too noisy.' The students looked at each other. They could have heard a pin drop. No one spoke. 'Too noisy', the guru said again. 'Too much chatter in the mind. We still have too many thoughts, feelings, opinions, judgements and disturbances. You cannot meditate until you have stopped the noise inside – and then you won't have to because, if you truly believe, things will happen.'

Karen Blixen, a Danish woman who came from her own country to Africa to start a new life illustrates this point nicely by quoting an example that was important to her about the power of belief. One day, shortly after she arrived, she was out hunting with friends when one of her African servants – who was tree-felling at the time – suddenly had his leg crushed by falling timber. Blixen says she heard the poor fellow moaning and rapidly made her way to him. When she reached the spot, she found that the lad was in terrible pain and he begged her to do something about it. Usually, Blixen carried lumps of sugar in her pockets to give to wounded animals but on this occasion she had nothing. The distressed native begged ever more earnestly that she should use whatever means she had at her disposal to relieve him of his pain and it was at this point that she remembered that the king of Denmark had recently sent her a royal letter in his own hand. As luck would have it, she was carrying it with her that day. Pulling the letter from her pocket, she told the wounded youth that a personal note like that from a king had almost magical powers. It could more or less take away all pain, however bad. She then laid the king's letter on the wounded boy's leg and held it in place with her hand. All night she continued with that same action and afterwards related how the words and the gestures she used had a powerful effect on the wounded youth. Somehow the thought of such a special letter seemed to give the lad courage and take away the worst of his pain.

From thence onwards, whenever any local person got very sick, Karen Blixen and her famous letter were always prized assets. The natives demanded to borrow the king's letter when dangerous situations arose because they believed something powerful would happen if they had it on their person. Because they believed, something usually did happen but not all prayer produces results so magically.

Many of the saints – most notably Teresa of Avila and Ignatius of Loyola – do not try to sugar the pill for 'beginners at prayer' with easy sentiments or false promises. Neither do teachers in seminaries or noviceships. I remember one of my own early instructors saying that we could expect to start our prayer lives with two years of consolation and then follow that up with 20 years of desolation. He believed that prayer was a slog, a slow process of pondering over searching and troublesome questions that creep up on most people at some stage in their lives. It takes time and effort to discover where Christ has been present and what the 'flow' of our lives has been over the past months. We shouldn't expect to find out too rapidly where moments or areas of consolation have been showing themselves, for it requires some discernment to discover where life, energy, enthusiasm, joy and peace have been manifesting themselves. In short, finding where God has been active in our lives is a task that cannot be rushed. In the same way, space and time are needed before we can work out where desolation, darkness of spirit and despondency have been making an entry. When we ask ourselves what has brought fear, discouragement, gloom and sadness to our lives, the answers and insights are likely to be slow in coming and the temptation is to look for, and expect, results immediately. If that's our expectation we are likely to be disappointed. With so much noise and clamour in today's culture, it is wise to carve out quiet periods so that self-awareness may be achieved. Such quiet spots are bought at a price. They may bring with them more than we bargained for. In the silence we may meet our greatest enemy, the one we fear most – ourselves – for involving ourselves in prayer means being present to what is happening around and within us. It is sometimes described in dictionaries as 'deep reflection' – being present to God in a deep and meaningful way. During this practice of 'being present', a number of layers of belief, as well as baggage we have carried around with us for years, may find themselves up for examination.

As we begin to meditate, differing moods, insights and nuances may make themselves known to us. These can be like a revelation – though perhaps less so to our friends and bystanders than to ourselves. What

communicates itself with difficulty to us may have been blatantly obvious to those who have had to view us from the outside over many years
and put up with our foibles. By listening to these revelations, our own
sense of ourselves may be sharpened. Our antennae may become more
finely tuned, and that fine-tuning is helpful. Sr Wendy Beckett, whom I
have already mentioned, goes so far as to say that spirituality encom-
passes the art of being present to ourselves and recognising what is
happening around and within us. She suggests that, during prayer, we are
a little like a fisherman at work. It may appear that we are doing nothing
but in reality a great deal is going on. Just as the fisherman keeps his eyes
peeled for the gentle ripple of wind across the face of a lake, or notices
how water swirls and eddies around particular shapes and formations in
the contours of the land, those engaged in spirituality are watching for
interior faith signs and signals. The fisherman maintains his alertness
because it helps his craft. In spirituality, the supplicant also is crafty,
trying to discern 'up and down' life moments. He or she tries to find the
'finger of God' or 'traces of the Spirit' in their daily living. They ask,
'what has lifted my spirit in recent days or – if they feel themselves in
desolation – 'what has deadened my spirit and sucked the energy out of
me'?

Initially, such degrees of self-awareness seem a tall order and so the
question immediately arises, 'Can anyone or everyone do it?' Well, ten
million American adults now say they practise some form of meditation
regularly so, given the right disposition, the answer is probably yes. We
are merely being asked to stay awake and stay aware in the hope that by
sitting in silence for half an hour or so each day, concentrating on a
breath or a word or an image, we might facilitate interaction between
God and our deepest innermost selves. Meditation is not really a matter
of forcing your mind to be quiet – it's more a question of finding the
quiet that is already there. Set aside time to go prayerfully over what has
been happening to you insofar as you have noticed. Link these happenings to the real world and the real you. Then find the interaction
between the two.

Thomas Merton, the Trappist monk, said 'meditation has no point
and no reality unless it is firmly rooted in life'. Its purpose is to enrich
human living and nourish life itself. It puts us in touch with our deepest,
innermost longings, fears and desires – close to the place where we are
likely to find God. Meditation is simply about being you and knowing
something about who that self is. It is about coming to realise that you
are on a journey whether you like it or not. Your life is the journey. Part

of what you seek is a realistic 'spirit' map to guide you on your way. Know that the journey is always unfolding and that, moment by moment, the terrain is constantly altering. What happens each moment influences what happens next, but you need to be watchful and ready. You have to come to this type of prayer at the right moment and at a point in your life where you are prepared to be attentive. On the temple portal in Delphi are the words 'Know Yourself'. We, too, need to regularly engage in personal stocktaking. Meditative prayer is our means to an end here insofar as it allows us to find a suitable rhythm for reflection and facilitates a meaningful, vibrant relationship with the living God. Pope John Paul II said that we achieve the fullness of prayer, not when we express ourselves but, when we let God be most present in prayer. Meditation has a lot to do with being intimate, not only with God, but also with your deepest self. Today, perhaps more than ever before, the necessity for finding time and space for God is paramount. As the material side of our lives flourish, a faint hint of unease may make itself apparent. Either individually or as a society we may detect that something of fundamental importance is absent. A 'lacuna' or blind spot may show itself. God may have faded from our picture.

One reflective and prayerful person put it to me like this: 'When I first learned to meditate, I felt fear. I was frightened to be alone with myself and fearful of looking into possible black holes and chasms within'. Many of us set up all sorts of diversions and distractions to cloud reality. We engage in daydreaming, frantic activity, sports and mind-games to escape a possible 'black hole' in our own lives, fearing that we might discover a lack of meaning or a lack of purpose in our lives. Observation of this sort is a skilled art. If you have ever watched sheep-dog trials on television, you are likely to be immediately struck by how diligently the dogs observe everything that is going on around them. They are only aware of the present moment. They stay fully alert, with eyes wide open and ears pricked. The situation presented to the dog is a constantly changing one. The sheep are in a continual state of motion and the dog tries to respond rapidly to any number of sensory clues that the animals emit. The dog-handler's job is to ensure that the dog stays completely present to every nuance. That is the habit we are trying to instil in ourselves during prayer for, within interior silence, we tend to get bursts of inspiration and all sorts of delicate emotions may come to the surface. A new awareness of what has been going on within is made conscious and what we feel about those happenings may also make itself manifest. Sometimes our very bodies will be our allies and will hint at interior goings-on, but the messages they send us are very subtle. The communication and shades of emotion they reveal can very easily be drowned out. They certainly will be unless we are careful to ignore the chronic roar and ceaseless chattering that constantly surround us.

Many things get in the way of our desire to meditate. We may be daunted by the hard work involved or by the apparent lack of results, or by the hoard of distractions that seem to take us over on every side. Oftentimes, our thoughts seem to wander all over the place right from the outset. In the east, they call this the 'monkey-mind' syndrome and prayer experts there liken our minds to a bunch of frantic monkeys who scamper among a tree's branches to amuse themselves. Like them, our minds find it hard to concentrate. Hindrances present themselves. The first of these can be common sloth or laziness. We know that, on a journey, an expedition cannot begin until the first step has been taken, but taking that first step can be damnably difficult.

Before setting out on a spiritual journey we may be beset by doubt and indecision. Many people are. Fr William Barry, the well-known American Jesuit, said that he personally finds it hard to get down to prayer and that numerous individuals have asked him why he bothers. In his writing, his answers are remarkably honest. Firstly, he admits, he prays because he's a priest and a Jesuit. It is expected of him. That, of course, is an answer he can't proclaim too loudly and so he goes on to explain that at times he has prayed mainly to placate God or because he needed a favour. You can almost feel from his answers that personal embarrassment is close to the surface. When pushed, his better nature comes to the surface and he simply says that he prays because he believes in a Saviour. Deep down he yearns for an interaction with the divine. 'I suppose I pray because my heart aches for God. Therefore, I try to let God know who I am and I ask God to reveal Himself to me'. His method of prayer is simple. He tells God what is going on in his heart and then waits to see if the Lord will respond in any way. Like St Ignatius of Loyola, he wants to know Jesus as fully as he can but this can only happen if he himself opens the depths of his heart to his Saviour. Perhaps what St Ignatius of Loyola said is true – that we were made for God and will not be happy until some form of communication exists between the one who created us and ourselves.

*

EXERCISE ONE
Preparatory Exercise

The great religions of the world, Christianity, Hinduism, Judaism, Islam and Buddhism to name but a few, all recommend meditation. The requirements of this type of prayer are silence, stillness, awareness and focus. During the prayer, you are attempting to be present to the now. You don't have to do anything. You just have to be. Usually, time given to such prayer helps you to get to know yourself better and to realise your gifts and talents. Sometimes it even helps you to see God in a new light. Meditating on – or resting with – Gospel stories generally gives us a better understanding not only of how Christ, while on earth, interacted with those around Him, but also tend to show up strengths and weaknesses within ourselves. Christ, as we see in the Gospels, is more than willing to help individuals who are prepared to help themselves so it's reasonable to suppose that He is equally willing to let them see the true desires of their hearts if they are prepared to be open with Him. That's certainly the premise I'm working on.

In your prayer space, begin to relax and ask for an intimate sense of God's presence as you pray. Endeavour to become aware of how you are, right at this moment. Empty your mind of day-to-day worries and allow yourself feel the emotions of people in the Gospels who had gone to see and hear Jesus. These people, from their Old Testament reading, knew that their Saviour was intimately connected with them and was the One who had known them from the first moment of their being. He was the Creator who loved them, gave them their first breath and held them in the palm of His hand. Make a small prayer now, and ask that as you pray, you might feel similarly cherished and secure. Try to imagine God looking at you and loving you, knowing the beauty that resides within. Let Him tell you of the gifts He sees in you. He knows the secrets of your heart and He senses your good times as well as your bad. Ask Him to accompany you when times are dark. Ask for courage in moments of doubt. Beg for light and warmth when things look bleak. Become conscious of anything in your life that disturbs you and ask that when such disturbing factors seem likely to overwhelm you, His spirit may give you a sense of empowerment.

*

Exercise Two
Preparing Yourself for Prayer

Let's try a short simple prayer exercise and see how we get on with it.

Go to the place you have selected and adopt a position that you will be able to hold comfortably for 20 minutes or so. Slow down. Be present. Breathe deeply. Try to be in touch with your feelings. Begin by becoming aware of your breathing. Breathe a little more deeply than usual and experience how this helps you to relax. Focus your awareness on your breath as it enters and leaves your body. Note how it is absorbed into your being and becomes part of you as you breathe inwards. Think about how this process is reversed when you begin to breathe out. Study the on-going rhythmical movement of your breathing as you draw the air deep into yourself and try to visualise this activity in your imagination.

Some people claim to have no imagination but, unless you are one of these, try to create an idea or picture in your imagination. I find it helpful to use fantasy to assist me with this task. I imagine that the room I am praying in is filled with a sort of coloured fog and as I breathe in, I try to see in my mind's eye this fog making its way into my body and slowly filling it up. It first enters through my nostrils and begins its journey down towards my innermost being.

As if you were watching the action on television, follow this coloured fog as it travels to the back of your throat and down into your shoulders. Now continue to observe – as if you had a glass torso – the coloured smoke as it moves into your chest area and thence circles down your backbone and makes its way into the very pit of your stomach. As this vision develops, just be aware. To assist the process, you might speak to yourself inaudibly and give yourself a running commentary on the actions taking place within you as you observe them. Next exhale. Allow the stale air make its way up from the pit of your stomach, circling up your backbone and coming back up towards your chest area. Imagine it as it moves up from your fingertips and comes back up to your shoulder area again before it is emitted from your throat and mouth back into the environment.

As you build up this quiet rhythm of breathing you may be further helped if you tell yourself that you are drawing in the peace of Christ on each inward breath. As you allow the stale air to escape, remind yourself that anything that has been disturbing, upsetting, frustrating or exhausting for you in the recent past is being taken away. Your prayer is that you are breathing peace quietly in and breathing tiredness gently out. Keep this process going for a minute or two and then calmly bring the exercise to an end.

This introductory breathing exercise can be a useful tool. Firstly, it slows us down and stills us. It may also open up a good place to engage Jesus and converse with Him. Breathe naturally and keep your attention on your breath pattern. On each inward breath, imagine that you give yourself energy. On the out breaths, imagine that you are letting go and releasing whatever prevents you from being calm within yourself. Between the in and out breaths, you may notice that a natural gap is created. Rest in that gap. Mystics in the east often say that our breath is our greatest friend and it is by focusing on the breath that inner relaxation and tranquillity – so helpful to prayer – are created.

As with most things, practice makes perfect. The sheer repetition of the above exercise usually begins to produce results. That's not to say that there won't be distractions. Treat these as you might deal with a puppy in training. In almost the same way as you might place a puppy on a piece of paper and encourage it to stay on the one spot, do the same for yourself. Just as the puppy will constantly move off the paper and in the early stages will need to be constantly returned to it, so too with yourself. As soon as you notice that you have strayed away from an awareness of your breathing pattern, gently bring yourself back and start again. Breathe normally. Keep the pattern light and easy. Do not force anything. You may notice that by paying attention to your breathing, you naturally tend to move deeper and deeper into relaxation and in this way become quieter. The brain relies on a plentiful supply of oxygen to do its work efficiently and the deep regular breathing that you are engaged in will calm your emotions and bestow tranquillity of mind. As you keep up a running commentary for yourself, 'now I'm breathing in, now I'm breathing out,' be aware that your pace of breath has slowed. Serenity has settled upon you. Well done. That's exactly what you're aiming for.

*

Exercise Three
The Burning Bush

Using the preparatory exercise outlined above, create an atmosphere of prayerful repose for yourself. Sit down and settle yourself. In this exercise you are trying to develop stillness and silence within yourself. Inner silence, if achieved and savoured, will bring long-term benefits. The quiet and peace achieved will give you strength to face any difficulties that life may send your way. In the silence of meditation you discover your gifts, hopes, dreams and beliefs and begin to see signs of God's presence around you. An old American poem suggest that every burning bush is alive with God but that only those who see the Divine take off their shoes. It's that sense of God all around us that we are trying to gain here.

When you are ready, imagine you are in a country place of great beauty. Possibly it's a place you know well. If you prefer to conjure up such a place from your imagination, feel very free to do so. In the Old Testament we are told that Moses went up a mountain and detected a burning bush. How exactly this manifested itself to him is not made particularly clear but it seems from the poetic lines quoted above that many who encounter such bushes see only the bush and nothing more. Very few take off their shoes or show any sign of reverence.

For a few moments, go back in your own mind over the last few weeks of your life and ask yourself whether any 'burning bushes' could possibly have lain across your path. Where could God possibly have re-vealed Himself to you? At first, if you are anything like the majority of us, you won't see God, His presence, or His actions very clearly. In a sense we are like the blackberry pickers. However, if you persevere, your understanding may begin to change. Perhaps God makes Himself pres-ent to us through other people or through events. Think of situations that you have found yourself in or people that you have met over the last month. Does any word, sentence or action from these individuals jump into your mind? Could it not be possible that God instigated such words or sentences and, through the encounter, found a way to reach your heart.

Finish by giving thanks for whatever revelations have been given to you.

When I work with students I try to tell them not to come out of meditation too quickly. Give yourself a 'settling down' period of a few moments. This creates a gap between the peace obtained during medi-tation and the flurry of everyday life. Don't jump up and rush off – blend the stillness into your normal existence.

*

Exercise Four
'Mary at the Tomb'
[John 20: 11–16]

First read the text of the Gospel story, as follows:

> Mary of Magdala was standing outside near the tomb, weeping. As she wept, she stooped to look inside and saw two angels dressed in white sitting where the body of Jesus had been, one at the head and the other at the feet. They said, 'Woman, why are you weeping?' 'They have taken my Lord away and I do not know where they have put Him'. As she said this she turned around and saw Jesus standing there, though she did not realise that it was Jesus. Jesus said to her, 'Woman, why are you weeping – who are you looking for?' Supposing him to be the gardener, she said, 'Sir, if you have taken Him away, tell me where you have put Him and I will go and remove Him'. Jesus said, 'Mary!'

Read through the text slowly a few times. What do you think the main point or question is? As I read the passage, I'm struck by the fact that Mary failed to identify Jesus, even though He was standing right beside her. The question I keep uppermost in my heart as I pray this passage is whether I, too, am equally unobservant in my faith life.

Take one more look at the text. This will mean that you do not have to consult it when you move into the meditation proper. It also offers you the opportunity of discovering new layers of meaning and implication as you work out what question might be most suitable for you to ponder. Think about what you really want to receive from God at this time and pray that the objectives you have in mind become a reality.

Start by concentrating on your breath and breathe naturally, focusing your attention on each inhalation and exhalation. As you breathe in, ask God to grant you peace of mind. When you breathe out, let go of all that disturbs you and release your tension. Between each inhalation and exhalation you will find there is a natural gap. Rest in that gap. Rather than watching the breath, identify gradually with the gap as if you were becoming it. Slowly the breath, the breather and the breathing become one. Become comfortable with your breathing pattern and make it your greatest friend. You will find that the slow rhythm of your inhalation and exhalation – if focused upon – will help you learn to relax.

Now conjure up the scene as it is depicted in the Gospel story. Place yourself alongside Mary Magdalene. Observe her in all her moods – solitude, isolation and sorrow. Why is she weeping? Ask her. She is remarkably honest by nature and will probably tell you that it's because her Lord and Master is dead but also because she is only too aware of her own failings. Is knowledge of her sinfulness the block to recognising Jesus? Let the Magdalene tell you herself. Perhaps it is her honest humility that finally allows the scales to fall from her eyes. It might not be a bad idea for me to ask her to help me remove the beam from my own eye.

At the end of the meditation, sit still and quietly survey what has happened. Does anything feel different from before you started? Realise that you have done something positive for yourself by mediating and that no matter what you may think has happened, you are going to take the benefits of the session away with you.

*

EXERCISE FIVE
A Fantasy Exercise: Making Friends with Yourself

Begin by zoning in your awareness towards your breathing pattern. Try to observe, in your imagination, your breath as it makes its way in and out of your body. Relax and settle down. Feel the sensation your breath makes as it flows naturally in and out. Help yourself by silently counting on each in-breath and doing the same as you allow each breath to escape. A slow, silent count of one, two, three, four, might suffice as you work on each of these inward and outward breaths. As each breath leaves the body, mark it with a mental count. As you sit there, begin to think about the body you have been given and the life you manage to live through it. How does it feel when you do that? Try to sense whether you feel joy or melancholy as you make your way through this exercise.

Work on developing a response of friendliness and kindness towards yourself. It might help if you use Juliana of Norwich's phrase, 'How lucky I am, how grateful I am'. Try to stay with that feeling of being grateful as well as lucky and if the emotion begins to diminish or evaporate, patiently work on bringing it back.

Now bring to the forefront of your consciousness the image of a good friend that you have known. Sketch an image of them into your mind and do this by recalling how they acted towards you in real life – say in a conversation, or an encounter, or an event. It's best if you choose someone who is around your own age and not someone who is much older or younger than yourself. Try to develop feelings of gratefulness and thanks towards them.

Next move on to someone who evokes more neutral feelings than the companion imagined previously. This will be somebody whom you neither like nor dislike strongly. At first you may not have any great feelings towards them at all. Try to stay, however, with whatever feelings actually come to the surface. Work on improving those bland feelings in a positive direction insofar as you can. Ask for good things to happen to the person you have in mind.

When you are ready, next turn your attention towards a person whom, in your opinion, you do not get on well with at all – a person who grates on you or someone who irritates you to a degree. Someone you dislike or who seems to think little of you. Become aware of the feelings that well up within you as you bring this person to the front of your imagination. You will probably make assumptions about how you think you will feel when their image comes into your imagination but stay with the feelings as they actually emerge. Insofar as you can, try to let go of any sense of acrimony and animosity that rise like bile to the surface. Such feelings are more likely to be harmful to you than to damage the person they are directed towards.

For the final stage of this meditation, try to situate all four characters (yourself, your good friend, the neutral persona and the loathsome individual) together into a group in your imagination. Your feelings and wishes for your friend will be warm and generous but try to conjure up good for the others too. Pray that the Lord will look favourably towards them all and gift them with His grace. Ask that good may come to the despised one as much as it may come to your friend. Keep this up for some little time.

When you are ready, gradually bring the meditation to an end. Don't bring the proceedings to a conclusion too abruptly, as this may jar your mood and leave you with an unpleasant sensation. Give yourself a few minutes quiet – as oasis of peace, as it were. Sometimes the fruit of such a meditation may take some little time to sink in and you may have to work assiduously to find out how it has affected you.

Seeing the Traces

CHAPTER 2

LEARNING ABOUT PRAYER

It is not the mountain we conquer but ourselves
— Sir Edmund Hillary

It's strange how people will travel long distances to visit a guru or master of prayer without being very sure what they are looking for. Many of those who came to Anthony de Mello were, it is true, interested in trying to improve their prayer lives but they also probably felt a little like St Augustine of Hippo. He was asked to explain the concept of 'time' and had to admit that he felt a bit stumped. He knew what time meant in a common-sense sort of way, but if you asked him to define the concept in exact terms, he had problems. His thinking became muddled and all his theories became a bit blurred.

Maybe those who came to de Mello had similar feelings when it came to their prayer life and their ideas about prayer. They had some rough idea what the word meant, but when it came to the specifics and their own prayer practice they became a bit vague. Fortunately, de Mello had some empathy with their dilemma. He believed there are many ways to pray and valued the fact that different traditions utilise a variety of aids and skills to support them in their task. The elements they use include the use of breathing, silence, visualisation, self-reflection and stillness, to name but a few, and de Mello himself used stories and parables to explain and illustrate faith practices to his listeners. One such story told of an Indian guru who was much renowned for his expertise in the field of prayer. People came from all directions to confer with him and many asked for tips about spirituality. They wished to discover what exactly they should do to achieve the best results. The guru, on being asked this question, was silent for some time before giving his pearl of wisdom. 'Just sit', he said. Now it has to be admitted that this answer didn't completely satisfy some of those who had asked the question for the guru himself seldom seemed to sit much. He was constantly on the go and spent much of his time moving about. In fact it was said that he even took up book-keeping chores in the monastery to keep busy, so his reply about being still both surprised and perplexed his questioners. 'Why, if that is the case, do you spend all your time in work?' they asked. The guru smiled quietly and replied, 'If you're smart enough, you can combine your work with inner stillness and meditation'.

Not many of us, however, can manage to combine activity and stillness easily. It seems that the average person has 60,000 separate thoughts each and every day. If that sounds a bit of a handful to you, don't despair. I've seldom met anyone who's seriously trying to pray who feels they are managing to achieve their aim without countless distractions. Similarly, none of those I've consulted feel they are giving sufficient time either to God or prayer. To tell the truth, if I met a person who did feel that their prayer practice was more or less perfect, I'd be inclined to take a second look and be highly suspicious. Cardinal Basil Hume, the late English primate, and a man I have great time for when it comes to the matter of prayer expertise, would, I feel sure, have felt equally unconvinced if people had told him that they managed to pray without difficulty. To illustrate the point that prayer requires commitment, he mentions in one of his books that if people only prayed when they felt like it, they would hardly ever pray at all. Also, he points out, that if we feel we are too busy to pray, we are busier than God wants us to be. Because of these factors, he recommends to his readers that they find a regular time and place to pray each day. Really, he points out, the only way to get into prayer practice is to get down and actually do it. Don't force yourself beyond your limits but start on a small scale. As your resolve grows stronger, build up your meditation time, little by little. In this way, slowly but surely, you will gradually be able to expand the duration of your sittings so that, after a month or two, you may be able to sustain the period of meditation for 40 minutes or so. Don't wait for some muse to appear, or for divine inspiration to strike, or for desperate circumstances to appear and bring you to your knees. Just start out. Begin wherever you find yourself. Most of us discover that knowing how to get started is one of our biggest quandaries.

So let's begin there. Choose a time of day that is right for you. Don't be too ambitious. You may be only able to manage five minutes initially. That's okay. Don't give up on the pretext that you can't find five minutes or that you can't find a place to be alone. Excuses are easy to find. Give whatever time you manage to chisel out to God and beg him to accept that. Offer him all your distractions as well as your dazzling insights. Try not to use the notion of 'distractions' as an excuse not to pray. Distractions are part of the experience. We can't escape them altogether but, as they say in India, 'Even though we can do nothing about the birds that fly around our head, we can stop them nesting in our hair'. In other words, try – insofar as you are able – to suppress whatever clamour is banging around inside your head. I mentioned that distractions are likely to invade your prayer space but maybe you can offer them also to God as part of your contribution.

I recall some time ago giving a workshop in Hawaii. Towards the end of my time there, one of the participants came to me with a beautiful sea-shell which she had obviously collected somewhere around the island. Before she handed it over, the director of the workshop stepped forward and explained that such shells were not easy to come by. In fact they could only be found in one particular spot on the island. This place was difficult to get at and quite a distance from where the conference was being held. I was embarrassed and began to protest that the giver shouldn't have gone to such trouble or walked such a length to obtain her gift. 'Long walk part of gift', was her simple answer when she handed the package over. In the same way, distractions are part of the prayer package and maybe are part of the offering we are trying to make to God. Don't let them divert you from your journey.

As you start out, try to create calm. Open up a space within yourself where you can talk with your God – and commune with your deepest self. It might profit us here to dwell again on the thoughts of Cardinal Hume for a while. Shortly before he died, the cardinal produced a book, which he whimsically entitled *Basil in Blunderland*. The title itself seems strange, but the cardinal, being very self-effacing, explained how it came about. He had first thought about calling his effort *Basil in Wonderland*, but began to think that if he used that title people might think that he knew what he was talking about. In fact we don't have to go very far into Hume's writings or lectures on prayer to discover that not only had he a profound knowledge of his subject but he also had the unusual ability to both simplify and entertain as he wrote. Most of his hints and advice are not only clear, but profound as well, and are sure to help us as we begin our prayer journey.

Like many a good teacher, Hume keeps things simple and direct. He begins with the question, 'When should one pray'? His answer seems to be: 'Whenever you can'. He himself prayed best in the early morning and experience had taught him that reflective praying is usually done best before the distractions of the day set in and choked him. So it may be with you. As the hours advance, it's usual for the day's affairs to gather momentum. Our minds become increasingly cluttered. At least that's the case for most of us and it was also for Cardinal Basil. He noted that as well as his attention being taken up with all sorts of mundane matters, the level of noise around him seemed to increase as his day wore on. Such noise and over-active lifestyle, is, he noted, less than helpful to most of us because prayer is normally helped by silence rather than by commotion. So, the first step for us will be to find a place.

Next step, find the time. Origen, the Christian theologian who died about 255 AD, was fond of commenting that any place can be suitable for prayer but, if you want to pray undisturbed, you would do well, if possible, to find a special place where some sort of solitude and seclusion is ensured. A consecrated place, so to speak. Perhaps such a place is given a holy atmosphere by the very fact that it is regularly prayed in. Taking time out in a place like this is a great help if we hope to recharge our batteries. We may be a little like the big yellow sunflowers that the artist, Vincent Van Gogh, was so enamoured with. They have an unusual habit. They close their petals each evening. It's as if they are taking time out from the world. They seem to need to turn inward for a while before turning outward again to face the world. Only when they have taken this period of seclusion can they resume the task God has given them. When the sun rises after their period of rest they spring into action and reopen their petals. They take up where they left off, and resuming their interaction with those around them. Our moments of prayerful solitude may fulfil a similar function.

For us to achieve these reenergising moments, we need first to situate ourselves in God's presence, or perhaps more accurately, become conscious that God is close by. Just as a battery, when plugged in, becomes recharged, so too may we become renewed during the time we allocate to prayer. It's not that we do nothing during this time – we in fact attempt to stay even more awake than usual. Pope John Paul II mentions in his writings that we require silence if we are to have any chance of perceiving God's action and presence in our lives, even if that silence can be demanding and a challenge to us.

Initially, in the moments of silence, we may appear to be doing very little but the truth is, in fact, quite the opposite. Though apparently virtually idle, much is going on below the surface. Like the swan that glides serenely over the surface of the lake with no apparent effort, much of the action is going on out of sight and below the surface. James A. Michener, the noted American author, used to say that character consists of what you do on the third and fourth try, so, during your time of prayer, watch for any signs or hints that your life story, or the prompting of the Spirit, may be laying before you. For example, how have you been feeling for the past few days? Have you even noticed? What has exhilarated or dragged you down? What fed your spirit? Where have you felt fully alive? You might like to take on an exercise to see how this works for you. Go over the last few days of your own life. How have you been? Have events told you anything about yourself? Who have you met? What trials or tribulations have you been through? Perhaps words of wisdom from other people or snatches of their conversation stayed with you? Do these remembered words or memories bring with them messages or intimations of inner movements that may have been going on within you?

Perhaps I might offer a gentle word of caution here. Don't be expecting anything too dramatic. The movements or signs you receive may be very subtle – almost like tiny ripples left on the surface of a pond by a gentle breeze. Alternatively, the given signs or hints may be major and quite clear, at least to others if not to ourselves. Our friends or acquaintances may see patterns of behaviour fairly clearly that tell them a lot. Ask them. We ourselves may not be as sharp-eyed or perceptive. We may ignore, reject, doubt or deny what seems to be staring us in the face. Ask yourself, 'Has any element of my prayer or of my life moved me recently?' Maybe I will get an insight from comments others have been making to or about me in the recent past.

This method of trying to stay awake and aware, noticing what is going on within our lives, is a method favoured by St Ignatius of Loyola. It is very realistic and down to earth. We are sometimes tempted to think that God resides somewhere in outer space, or is to be found mostly in Church buildings or during religious services. I think it may be rather more accurate to believe that God is with us at all times and in every situation. As it says in Genesis (28:16), 'God was in this place, and I knew it not'.

To realise that we may be missing sightings and hints of God's presence, take time out. For many of us, elements of the contemplative life are a necessity, at least at times. Such time away from our daily routine provides space. It means we can be present to what is happening around and within us, regardless of how we feel. We don't have to be a hermit to achieve such space and Anthony de Mello mentioned this often enough. He talked, on occasion, about an easy-going disciple of an Indian guru who had problems achieving inner silence. This man complained that he never experienced the stillness his master spoke so eloquently about and he was both surprised and bothered by this. He was told that silence only comes to active people who work for it. We need to go to the trouble of carving out periods of quiet for ourselves.

But we cannot stay hidden in these cocoons of silence forever and de Mello also liked to point this out. As with so many points, he also illustrated this with one of his Indian guru stories. He spoke of a spiritual director who had advice for people who prolonged their stay at the monastery. Sooner or later each of them would hear the master's insightful tones directed towards them and they were informed that the moment had come for them to leave because if they did not depart, the Spirit would not come. Usually this message put the disciples' noses a little out of joint and they badgered the master about who this Spirit might be. In reply they were told:

> Water remains alive and free by flowing.
> You will remain alive and free by going.
> If you do not get away from me you will stagnate and die
> And be contaminated.

It takes courage to risk leaving the familiar. In the stillness that prayer may afford you, ask God for help in understanding what goes on at an interior level in your life. At first, not much of interest may make itself known to you. Try, however, to persevere in your task of soul-searching, even if at first you may not be exactly sure what to do. Some intuitive people utilise a style of inner probing that might be described as something like a person who wanders along a beach, waiting to see what the sea will wash up. Much – but not all – of what comes into their vision is useless flotsam and jetsam. Ideas float around, images come and go, but occasionally significant messages and perceptions about their inner self begin to display themselves. God may be bringing what lies submerged to the surface.

God may be revealing to us aspects of ourselves hitherto unknown or unsuspected and He may be doing so for a good purpose. Meditation often purifies the ordinary mind, unmasking distortions and illusions and in that way helps us recognise who we really are.

Look, listen, learn – and if the golden moment of revelation occurs, give thanks. It is His gift. If, on the other hand, such golden moments do not occur, be grateful that your prayer is still most pleasing to God. If the self-discoveries do not come thick and fast, the temptation to give up may be almost overpowering. It's at this point that we need to stick around and remain involved if we are to achieve the desired results.

Sheer perseverance is what's called for here.

I am reminded of a scene from *Alice in Wonderland* where a character called Dodo is introduced to us. He has the characteristic we're after in abundance. In the novel, Dodo and some of his friends managed to get themselves soaking wet during some bad weather. As each stood soaked and miserable, they asked how they might dry off. Dodo's suggestion was that a 'caucus' race should be held. When the friends asked what a 'caucus' race was – and why they should engage in it – Dodo answered that the best way to explain was to get the whole business of the race underway. They needed to participate. A little like prayer really. The race began. Everyone started running when they felt like it, and left off when it pleased him or her. Suddenly Dodo called out that the race was over. The friends asked who had won and Dodo, who had started the whole proceedings, maintained that everyone had won and that all should have prizes. Indeed, it could truthfully be said that they were winners, for by this time, all had managed to get themselves warm and dry. They had fulfilled their original intention.

We could say the same about the race of life organised by God. The hope is that everyone perseveres and wins. But – and this is quite essential – you have to be involved in the race to get your prize. You must take part. It's hard to see how God can open a door for us if we do not leave one at least a little ajar. In our participation, things will at times go wrong for us. In *Alice in Wonderland* terms, we'll get wet and question why. We'll argue and bicker and demand answers and sometimes be met by an apparent wall of silence. In fact, God usually does answer, but in His own way and in His own time. His way may be unexpected and the insights offered are easily overlooked by the impatient seeker. Learn to be tolerant. One old retreat-giver, when asked how he prayed and waited upon God's answer, said, 'Speak to the Lord in your own words and ask Him to lead you. Keep your prayer simple. Talk to God as to a father, to Christ as to a brother, and to the Holy Spirit as if He were a constant companion. Do not be too impatient. You may have to go on for week after week pleading and begging. Despite your entreaties, it may often seem that the Lord is unheeding.' We might take heart from that same retreat master, who – speaking from personal experience – related that God often came to him mysteriously. 'All I can say is that in my case I am filled, after prayer, with a peace I have not known before. Perhaps in that peace is the answer I am looking for'.

Regularly, in the Gospels, we note that Jesus recommends that we pray diligently for He has told us repeatedly that God listens. Why then, does the Father sometimes seem to make prayer so difficult? I'm not sure, but it may be because struggle itself, when engaged in, makes breakthroughs all the sweeter when they are granted. God allows us to experience the low points of life to teach us lessons we could not learn in any other way. Remember how farmers hope for lots of rain right after they plant their corn. Once the crop is in the ground they then hope for a dry period. They reckon the dryness will force the corn's roots to grow downwards in search of water, rather than stay on the surface. Unless the root of the corn grows downwards towards the water level, the corn will wither and die as soon as the heat of summer sets in. Our prayer may be a bit like that. God usually gives us an easy start but then sometimes allows long dry spells to occur. These fallow patches force our prayer roots to grow downwards. We are driven to reach deeper levels of faith rather than remain at surface level where not much is demanded of us.

Our spirituality may take a giant leap towards maturity when we cease being over-concerned about God's presence, especially at times of prayer. The temptation for most of us is that we always want to feel God close at hand and we become dejected when He withdraws His face from us. We search for certainty. We want to be sure that God does exist. If that kind of assurance came automatically with prayer, everybody would be at it. You would not need faith at all, just the logical ability to work out the existence of God in your head. And the head, as de Mello says, is not a particularly good place to be if you are trying to deepen your prayer life. It may not a bad place to start, but if you stay there among the clouds too long it becomes more and more difficult to reach the heart level. If that is allowed to happen, then your prayer is likely to become dry and frustrating. Not only that, but if we fail to move out of the head area and refuse to move toward the heart then our prayer is likely to become just a duty. Our direction should be towards the area of feeling, sensation and loving. This is where contemplation resides, the area where prayer can become a transforming power.

God has chosen to make us all different and so, for our part, we must try to seek out a prayer pattern best suited to enhance our relationship with the Almighty. Sometimes finding such a pattern this takes years to appreciate. Basil Hume, the English Benedictine I've quoted before, noted that the prayer model held out to him in his youth did not seem to fit easily into his particular personality make-up. Quite simply, for him, it didn't work. He says that in his own case it took time to discover the prayer method most suited to him – one that was in tune with his general lifestyle – and one that appealed more to the heart than the head.

So what prayer style suits you or me? It seems that we may have to experiment before we can say for certain. It may even be that different styles or methods will suit us at different times of our lives. Faith is a gift from God and so trying to develop a bond between God and us may be mostly God's work but that doesn't preclude us from doing our bit. Building up the relationships can be slow and ponderous but we may derive encouragement by thinking about the work of Theodore Elliott, an engineer, who, in 1848, began work on the Melrose Suspension Bridge. This project was an attempt to link the United States with Canada, close to the Niagara Falls. As the waters running around the rapids were fast and furious, Elliott pondered for quite some time about how he would hook a line between one side and the other. He could not swim between the two riverbanks as the waters ran too swiftly and he was unable to row the distance for the same reason. Something subtler was needed. First of all a kite was flown across the river with a tiny thread attached to it. When workmen on each bank had this thread in their hands, they attached a length of cord, and, by means of the thread, gently hauled the cord across. After this, a rope was tied to the end of the cord and the process was repeated. Only then did Elliott attach a cable of wire to the rope and drag the whole line across. The first point of contact had been very delicate and fine. The link between the two sides, which began with a tiny thread, was developed and made strong through progressive stages. By such means the objective was achieved.

Our contact with God may also begin in very delicate ways. From tiny beginnings a firm link or bond may be developed stage by stage. Often it's hard to know what might be useful. Many stratagems may be used to strengthen this bond as Abraham Lincoln, the American President, discovered. The point was brought home to him when, as a lawyer, he visited a former client. This lady was on her deathbed and asked him to draw up her last will and testament and, as he did so, the sick lady asked Lincoln to hasten her path to God by reading a few passages from the Bible. The future president wasn't expecting this request but he began to recite from memory the lines 'The Lord is my shepherd'. This seemed to have the desired effect. Shortly afterwards the woman died peacefully and the onlookers commented with some surprise that Lincoln had acted as both pastor and attorney. As the future president put it himself, 'You never know what will strengthen the bond between a person and God. All I know is that God and eternity were very near to me at that moment'.

Make use of whatever opportunities are given to you to strengthen or reawaken the bonds between God and yourself. Try not to let them pass by unnoticed. Most of us think that our feeble attempts at prayer must be about the worst possible examples of the art ever seen but if we stop and listen to others we will be re-assured. Almost everybody feels that those around them make better attempts to pray than they do themselves.

This was brought home to me some little time ago when a group of Jesuits on retreat began to discuss their own prayer attempts. The first individual mentioned that he tried to still himself and be silent from the outset. He stressed that, though he did speak and initiate conversations with the Lord, he also tried to create space within which he could listen. He felt it important to allow God the chance to speak – otherwise the interaction became very one-sided. Different Jesuits related in turn how they tried to interact with God, and a multitude of prayer styles began to emerge. The second contributor mentioned how he looked to those around him to provide some kind of mirror to God. In a sense he felt God was speaking to him through his companions. The third Jesuit pinpointed a different approach for he used a phrase made famous by a well-known Irish writer, Brendan Behan, who, when asked whether or not he was a Catholic, replied that he was a night-time Catholic. By that he meant that he only prayed when he felt himself to be in deep trouble, or, as he put it himself, in the dark. Similarly, this third Jesuit said that he noticed God's presence most acutely in times of pain, sadness, turmoil, tragedy, or when he was up against a blank wall – or appeared to be – in his relationship with God. This seemed to happen at times when he found himself with plenty of questions, but no answers. The fourth speaker noticed God's presence most clearly in nature. He sensed the beauty of God as he walked by the seashore or on mountain hikes, or when he was captivated by sunsets that brought an end to long hard days. Contrasting prayer styles suited these different individuals at various stages of their existence. So what style of prayer might best bring a sense of God's presence to you?

Some say that praying, for them, goes through four phases. First, they talk at God, even if this allows the Almighty little opportunity to respond. Then, when they feel able, they shift focus and talk to God. Next, they listen to God and finally – though this may take some time – they get to the point where they listen for any intimation of God in their lives. They try to be aware of God as He reveals Himself to them. They savour the richness, feel the pain, acknowledge the tedium of their own lives, and try to stay in the present moment. One of my own theology professors used to say that prayer for him was a matter of prayerfully reflecting over what was going on in his life on a daily basis. You needed to act like a cow, chewing the cud in a field. You take the events of the day and go over them piece by piece. You notice what happened and try to recognise where God may have been active in your life. Take each little happening, and – as it were – chew over what emerges. Stay with each incident until you have slowly chewed the goodness out of it. You may not, perhaps, be able to suck all the goodness from the event that it actually contains, but at least you may be able to gain all that is present for you at this moment in time.

*

Exercise One
Getting Ready for Prayer

Anthony de Mello, as we have seen, encouraged brief exercises for achieving inner silence. He wanted his listeners to obtain the revelation that silence brings. For this he suggested taking up a comfortable posture, closing our eyes, and then keeping silence for a period of ten to fifteen minutes. Initially, we have to soak ourselves in the silence and – having obtained it – immerse ourselves in whatever revelations it brings. At the end of de Mello's own exercises, participants were invited to open their eyes and share the experience with their companions. They would tell each other, insofar as they felt able, what they had experienced during the time of silence. It can sometimes be helpful for participants to take a few minutes on their own with a pen and reflection sheet to jot down what emerged for them personally before getting down to any shared talk.

*

Exercise Two
The Three Wise Men

Close your eyes and begin to take note of how you are breathing. Watch the pace of your breath, and how deep you are drawing it inside yourself. To help you with this activity, imagine that the place you are praying in is filled with a coloured fog. Select a colour that seems pleasing and calming to you. With each breath you draw inside yourself, imagine that the coloured fog is coming into your body. Note it as it comes first to your nose, then to the back of your throat, and afterwards down to your shoulders, arms and down to the tips of your fingers. See it also as it makes its way down to your chest area, circles around your back-bone and then is drawn down to the very pit of your stomach. Allow the pace and rhythm of your breathing to calm you and give you a sense of peace. Try to keep your posture erect, as a hunched or slouched position will restrict your breathing.

As you close your eyes, you may begin to see lights and images flashing in your mind's eye. As you relax, try to sketch a picture into your imagination in much the same way as you might visualise a story by means of a movie. In your imagination, see the story unfold before you. The story you are trying to conjure up is the well-known Christmas one of the Three Wise Men. We know from tradition that they are astute and reflective. They have seen something in their own country that has perplexed them. Clearly the experience they have undergone must have been something stupendous, for to undertake an expedition such as the one they are now on would not be attempted lightly. Be with them as they leave their families. Imagine the doubt and scorn they have to face. Supposed to be wise, they are starting a journey without any clear idea about where they are headed or how they will be guided. The risks will be great and the rewards uncertain, if they come to fruition at all. They will hear the questions from their families and friends ringing in their ears asking them why they could not put such foolish plans and dreams out of their minds and stay at home where they were needed and safe.

Yet still they started out. What faith! What courage!

Follow them in your imagination as they trudge along carrying their gifts for a king whom they had never met. They wanted to offer the finest gifts (i.e. talents) they had at their disposal. Think for a moment about your own gifts and your own generosity of spirit. What, in your estimation, are those gifts and how much do you want to offer them to Christ?

Next think of how slowly the Wise Men had to search for their objective. Without the certitude they craved, they must have stopped long and often to pick up whatever tips they could from people along the way. Few would have knowledge about what the special star in the sky could mean. The Wise Men were not taking the motorway route, fast and smooth, and with an asphalt surface. Rather they were taking a secondary or byways route, badly marked and uncertain. Even the pace at which they travelled would have been constantly interrupted by the necessity to take sightings and mileage checks. These men were travelling in hope rather than expectation – just as many are doing on the 'Faith Trail' today; stumbling along, without the apparent doctrinal certainty offered by ecclesiastical establishments of yesteryear. Meandering along on their own, well away from formal churches or recognised ministers. Pause here for a moment to pray for individuals such as these – people who are trying to make their way forward in faith under enormous clouds of doubt or uncertainty. The Wise Men did not only have to contend with natural hazards along their route: there were those who wished to actively frustrate them from achieving their goal. For a moment, concentrate your gaze on the figure of Herod. He would have heard about the star and about the rumours of a king's birth in his locality. He was an obstacle to the Wise Men on their search. Are there people or situations that are actively hindering me in my faith journey? If so, what are they and what can I do – or what do I need to do – about them?

Despite all opposition, the Wise Men did reach their objective and gave thanks for Christ's existence and presence in their lives. Now take a few minutes for yourself so that you might give thanks to the Wise Men for their courageous expedition and pray that, just as they delivered their gifts to the Christ-child, so also Jesus might shower His gifts upon you.

*

EXERCISE THREE
The Appearance on the Shore of Tiberias
[John 21:1–12]

Later on, Jesus revealed Himself again to the disciples. It was by the Sea of Tiberias, and it happened like this: Simon Peter, Thomas called the Twin, Nathaniel from Cana in Galilee, the sons of Zebedee and two more of his disciples were together. Simon Peter said, 'I'm going fishing'. They replied, 'We'll come with you'. They went out and got into the boat but caught nothing that night. As soon as it was light, they noticed Jesus standing on the shore, though they did not realise that it was Jesus. He called out, 'haven't you caught anything, friends?' and when they answered, 'no', he said, 'throw the net out to starboard and you'll find something'. So they threw the net out and could not haul it in because of the quantity of fish. The disciple whom Jesus loved said to Peter, 'It is the Lord'. At these words, 'It is the Lord', Simon Peter tied his outer garment round him (for he had nothing on) and jumped into the water. The other disciples came on in the boat, towing the net with the fish; they were only about a hundred yards from land.

As soon as they came ashore they saw that there was some bread there and a charcoal fire with fish cooking on it. Jesus said, 'Bring some of the fish you have just caught'. Simon Peter went aboard and dragged the net ashore, full of big fish, one hundred and fifty-three of them; and in spite of there being so many the net was not broken. Jesus said to them, 'Come and have breakfast'. None of the disciples was bold enough to ask, 'Who are you?' They knew quite well it was the Lord.

Go to a quiet place and clear your mind. Use one of the breathing exercises to settle the chaos within. Take your time. If distractions occur, note them but don't get too worried. Just bring your attention back to the subject matter at hand. When you are ready, read the passage above. Then with your eyes closed, allow yourself enter the meditation.

Visualise the scene. It's very early morning, just as dawn is breaking, and you are in a little boat with some of the Lord's disciples. How do you think they are feeling? Remember that their master and chief hope has been savagely taken from them just days before. It's likely an aura of gloom surrounds the scene. Suddenly a figure appears on shore. How long has He been watching over events? How long has He been disturbed by the pain of His followers? He has the hopes and aspirations of the others at the forefront of His concern. Has He also got the same concern for me? Stay with that thought for as long as it seems profitable. Remember that in the Gospel scene it takes a little time for the disciples to work out who the character on shore is. Who – or what – tells them it is the Saviour? At times of distress in my life, have I recognised Christ on my shore? Have I ever felt His deep concern for my tribulations? If the answer is yes, how did that concern manifest itself and have I thanked Him for it? If no, had I simply got my eyes shut?

Stay with the scene for a little while before bringing the meditation to a close.

CHAPTER 3

GETTING A SENSE OF YOUR OWN WORTH

If you don't believe in yourself, who the hell will?
– Tom Clancy

Most people have heard of Thomas Edison. Among many other things, he invented the light bulb. It's said that he was also a hard but fair task-master and some of his young assistants were fond of telling a story that may make your hair curl. It certainly had that effect on his employees. One day, when Edison was making the final improvements to his first light bulb and had almost produced the perfect article, a significant event occurred. The day's work was drawing towards its close and Edison called one of his youngest helpers across to him. He asked the lad to carry the almost completed light bulb to an upstairs storeroom so that it could be deposited safely for the night. The youngster nervously carried the precious object step by step up the stairs but at the very last moment he stumbled. To the horror of the other assistants standing around, the newly created bulb was dropped. Needless to say, it smashed. This meant that Edison and his whole team had to work for another 24 hours to make a new one.

The next day, as they came towards the end of producing the new bulb they were horrified to see Edison calling the same youth across and entrusting their creation to his unsteady hands. On this second occa-sion, the storing job was completed successfully. Edison's gesture prob-ably changed the boy's life. It certainly gave him a sense of his own worth. Edison knew that there was more than a light bulb at stake here for he sensed that his young assistant, like many others, had a fragile sense of his own value and worth. By asking the young man to re-attempt the assignment, Edison was showing that he had not lost faith in him. He was, in a sense, engaging in a Christ-like gesture – he was giving the lad back his sense of self-worth.

Consider, for a moment, how Christ deals with those around Him,

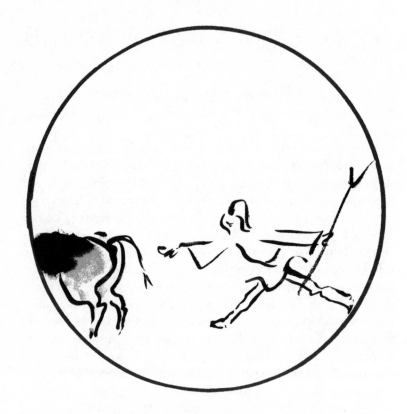

Seeing the Ox

particularly those with fragile self-belief. Mary Magdalene may serve as a perfect example. Everybody knew she was a sinner and Christ cannot have been unaware of this. Mary herself knew her shortcomings, but Christ was determined to give her a sense of her own value. Each one of us needs a mentor like that – someone who will build-up and revitalise us.

I remember one small boy who attended a boarding school telling a story about his first visit to the school infirmary. The lad was very young at the time and had a badly misshapen back since birth. To say that he was conscious of his deformity would be an understatement. On that first visit, the doctor sensed the boy's lack of self-confidence and said to him, 'Do you believe in God?' When the answer came back in the affirmative, the doctor told him that the more you believe in God the more you believe in yourself. Then he took the boy's medical chart and in the column describing physical characteristics he jotted down, 'this boy has an unusually well-shaped head'. The wording was beautiful in its simplicity. As the young lad told this story many years later, he said he had been taught a lesson he would never forget. If you believe in God, and focus on the best in yourself, nothing can defeat you. You have to believe in yourself, for, as Tom Clancy asks in one of his books, 'If you don't believe in yourself, who the hell will?' Not only have you to believe in yourself but you also must take care of yourself – because you never know when the world will need you or your talents. To believe in yourself you first have to find out who you are, but how is this to be done? Perhaps you gain this knowledge partly through taking time out to be self-aware and to find out where your drives come from.

Various sources suggest that, broadly speaking, there are two different types of individuals. The first type is energised by activity and by human interaction. The other human type is more introspective – deriving energy more from the inner world of ideas than by engaging with humanity and outer activity. So, in almost all cases, introverts and extroverts are driven onwards and gain their energy from different stimuli. It's rare for an individual not to adhere to these norms though in the case of Christ, being God and man, He is unique. He seems to combine the attributes of introvert and extrovert and is, in a sense, a contemplative in action for it's almost impossible to pin Him down to one category. As we observe Jesus when reading the Gospel, he seems, at times, to be the centre of attention – the one around whom the action rotates. On other occasions He is surprisingly alone and isolated, very much off by Himself. He constantly appears to find time for solitude, knowing that He needs it. Alone, He takes time out to focus on what He is about – His

Father's business. Following Christ's example, we might model ourselves on His behaviour if we wish to maximise our potential.

Krishnanurti, the eastern mystic, says something similar. Asking how a person might find out who they are, he suggests that the task can be done most easily in relationships and communication with others. Stillness and silence do help, but the value of interaction with others should not be under estimated. Their comments force us toward self-examination and their insights often highlight hidden aspects of ourselves that we may have overlooked. They view us from different perspectives and examine our behaviour from new and unusual vantage points. They can mirror back to us how we are projecting ourselves to the world.

But a cautionary note should be added here. Such comments must be treated with wariness, as they are not always positive or helpful. They often disturb us, sometimes in a good way, but sometimes destructively, as de Mello was fond of pointing out. He talked about an Indian friend of his who bought his paper each morning from a particularly cranky newspaper-vendor. This hawker had the habit of handing out a grumpy or disparaging remark along with each broadsheet he disposed of. Friends asked why the buyer should choose to go to such a distributor and he answered that he was damned if he was going to allow the comments of others – wholesome or hostile – to determine how he would feel during his day. In essence we should not allow the actions of others, or their comments, to disturb us unduly.

Borrowing from his own experience, de Mello recounted how he had, on one occasion, seen a father and son aboard an Indian train. The boy was about 12, and was in a conversation with his father, when the train's ticket-collector came into the private compartment where they both sat. The conductor was about as rude as you can imagine and began to ask roughly for their tickets. When the father produced two tickets the inspector turned really nasty. He accused the father of having only a child's ticket for the boy and complained that the lad certainly didn't look like he qualified for a juvenile fare. This haranguing match went on for some minutes but, despite all provocation, the father remained calm. Finally, the inspector punched the tickets and gruffly departed. As soon as he had left, he boy began to remonstrate with his father complaining that the inspector had been rude and arrogant and should not have been allowed get away with such behaviour. He wondered why the father had let the matter go unchallenged. The father's reply was short and simple. 'Ah, God help him. We only have to put up with his peculiarities for a few minutes. The poor man has to put up with himself all day.'

Not many of us can remain undisturbed no matter what life throws at us. The smallest negative comment – about our appearance, our abilities, or our humour can knock us completely out of stride. Despite the fact that we know in our hearts a good deal about where our strengths and weaknesses lie, it does not take much to puncture our confidence. Try to know clearly who you are – warts and all.

In the Gospels, Christ asked his friends, 'Who do people say that I am?' He didn't need to ask the question. He knew. The question was asked to help the disciples. We, however, might not be so confident about our own identity. You might like to try a prayerful exercise at the end of this chapter that will help you with self-clarification for it is called, 'Who are you?' This kind of prayerful meditation is also an awareness exercise. It helps you to observe yourself.

At first, observing yourself and your responses to various situations may seem artificial and difficult. With time and practice, it becomes natural and easy. Try it for a short period.

I studied group-work, i.e. the way people interact, while at college. We were regularly given an exercise to do, which proved to be beneficial. We were asked to notice what people got up to while they were in a pub. This method of studying human behaviour became a reflex action after a while. Patterns of behaviour were observed. Soon they became easy to spot. It helped that the patterns were repeated over and over during an evening. This helped foster an awareness of what was going on around us. It also meant that we could notice recurring modes of behaviour – even our own.

Once these patterns were noticed, it became possible to consider changing them. So stop and look at yourself. Notice how you are acting and reacting at any given moment. Through self-observation you may come to moments of insight. Jesus did this for His disciples. At regular intervals he invited them to come away to a quiet place. For this type of self-awareness, you need a certain amount of aloneness.

The exercise outlined above – when mulled over in a prayerful fashion – may help focus and reveal the real me to myself.

In the east they tell a story about a seeker after truth who visited a guru and asked to be told the truth about himself. He heard that if he wanted to know the real truth there was only one thing he must possess: not, as he supposed, an overwhelming passion for truth, but rather an unremitting readiness to admit that he might be wrong. If, through self-knowledge, we find we have to change aspects of ourselves, we must be ready first for a certain amount of suffering.

Leo Tolstoy said that when it comes to change, people are remarkably similar to each other for they all want to change humanity, but are not particularly keen on changing themselves.

To strive for change – and achieve it – a number of prerequisites are necessary. We first have to know that aspects of our own selves may be damaged. Once this fact is acknowledged, the possibility of repair begins to loom on the horizon. First we ascertains what area we are damaged in before putting strategies for regrowth into place. The conditions and the timing must be right. We rush around so much that before we can see what might need repairing we require a period of tranquillity. This breathing-space allows our inner spirit catch up with the rest of us and so a chance for change begins. God wants to help. He does, however, require a little assistance from us. If it were not so, we would become infantile and immature in our prayer practice. We do not want to be like the individual they speak about in the east who went to a religious convention. As soon as he went into the marquee where the convention was being held, he proclaimed loudly that he had such great faith in God that he had left his camel untied outside the tent. 'Go back out and first tie up your camel, you fool, for God does not have time to do for us what we can easily do for ourselves,' he was told. Or like the holy man who had great faith in God's ability to look after him at every turn. One day, bad weather came to this man's region and local police came around advising all to move to higher ground. Floods were expected. The holy man was unperturbed. He insisted he would stay in his house as he had complete confidence that God would look after him no matter what the weather was like. Rains came, and the water level rose. The fire brigade came around offering to transport people to safer ground but our holy man remained in his home. He was adamant that God would look after him. Despite his confidence the rains continued to pour down unabated. The waters now rose to second floor level in most houses in the district and the holy man was the only one who remained in place. Finally, a helicopter was sent to pluck him from his rooftop, as the floodwaters had now reached that level. The holy one told the helicopter crew that God would certainly look after him as he had such great faith and so the chopper took off to see if any remaining stranded citizens needed assistance. Still the waters came and finally they engulfed the house, drowning the holy man. When he arrived at the pearly gates, he demanded to know why God had left him unattended and in the lurch, despite his great faith. It's said that God looked perplexed and couldn't really understand what had happened because, as God Himself said, 'First I sent you the police, then the fire-brigade, and finally a helicopter to assist you out of your dilemma'. At times we need to use common sense and be pro-active. We need to help ourselves and do what we can about our own dilemmas before throwing ourselves on God's mercy.

When we try to help ourselves we may find that there are blockages within us which make us 'stick' in certain areas of our lives. The patterns that have begun to emerge through our self-observation hopefully contain some positive characteristics but it's highly probable that they have some unhelpful aspects as well. Wise people will begin to ask themselves, 'Where am I stuck?' What areas of my life have not been producing good fruit over the past year? What 'sticks' me? Am I stuck by old rules and, if so, what might this mean?' The notion of being stuck or blocked in quite a variety of ways is a difficult one to accept and the questions outlined above are a sort of checklist that might help me to take the next positive step forward in my life. So in what way might I be stuck?

I remember some years ago visiting a circus ground in Ireland. I was struck by the fact that a number of elephants waited passively around, just waiting for something to happen. All the elephants – both big and small – had a chain around their legs, which was attached to a post in the ground. One or two of the elephants were very small and their chains would certainly have held them in place but the bigger elephants, surprisingly, had the same size of chain assigned to them. In their case, they looked as if they had more than enough power to pull the post out of the ground – but they never did so. The elephant trainer explained that all elephants in his care were chained like this from a very young age. Their memories had taken on a sort of mind-set. They were convinced that the chain would hold them in place – and so it did. However, as years went by, the elephants changed in physique. They got bigger! Now the larger elephants could easily have pulled their chains away from the tethering pole if they used any force. However, because of the mind-set they had built up, and even more because they permitted this mind-set to remain fixed, they allowed the chains to limit their horizons. Once upon a time, because of their immaturity, they had not been able to break free. Now, despite their new circumstances, they no longer attempted to break loose from their chains. Old rules – which in fact no longer applied – continued to tie them down.

A second way we might be stuck is through fear. Years ago, while working in Africa, I had occasion to visit an open-air animal park. One exhibit that attracted a lot of attention was a large snake known as a boa constrictor. It resided in a fair-sized pit, which had wire netting all around to prevent the snake's escape. A sign nearby announced that the snake was fed daily at 1p.m. by its keeper. I arrived at the snake pit just before mealtime and joined the throng who wanted to see the snake being put through its paces. Right on the stroke of one the keeper appeared with a live rabbit under his arm. He proceeded to fling this live rabbit over the wire netting and it landed right in the middle of the snake pit about six feet from where the snake waited. Immediately the reptile seemed to rear up on its tail, standing upright like a walking stick. Its head and large neck swayed in a mesmerising fashion from side to side. The poor rabbit, quivering through fear like a bowl of jelly, remained transfixed before its gaze. It was at this point that I noticed that the circular wire fence surrounding the pit had a small hole at its base. I admit that the gap was tiny, and would not have allowed the large, bulbous neck of the snake to wiggle free, but the tiny rabbit could, as far as I could see, have affected its escape if it had made a dash for freedom. Instead it remained in place, rooted to the spot through fear, and after a few seconds the snake's head darted downwards and gobbled up the rabbit for lunch. I'm not certain the rabbit could have run away if it had made a bolt for it, but it seemed to many onlookers that fear prevented it even contemplating such action. So it can be with us.

A third way we might find ourselves stuck is through memories of past failures. I remember on one occasion an American animal behaviourist telling a story against himself which illustrates the point nicely. The American remembered how he had brought his young son fishing one day and they managed to land a small trout. The young lad was delighted and insisted that they put their catch in a bucket of water to bring it home. There, the behaviourist had a fish-tank that happened to have only one inhabitant – a small but robust pike. As the behaviourist himself put it, 'In a moment of madness I popped our recent catch in with this predator. Within moments, the inevitable happened. The pike devoured the little trout. I don't have to tell you that the young son was devastated. He was so upset that the father had to promise that they would again go fishing the following day to catch a replacement. Next day, they went and caught a small minnow. The father was determined that it should not meet the same fate as its predecessor. He searched his house and in the garage found a suitably sized piece of glass sheeting. Waiting until the pike was up one end of the fish tank, he jammed this piece of glass as a divider down the centre of the tank. This split the watery space into two distinct halves. He then popped the minnow into the empty half of the tank. For a moment all was quiet. Then the pike, seeing a new meal had arrived, made a headlong dash to consume it. It bashed its nose against the glass-divider. Apparently rather shaken, it retired to brood over its misfortune before making a second lunge for the minnow. Again the glass divider intervened and another sore snout resulted for the pike. All that day the father noted that the pike made repeated attempts to get at the small minnow but each time the divider repelled it. By nightfall, it had finally got the message. Failure imposed its own rule. The pike finished making its headlong dashes towards its intended victim as these attempts always ended in a bloody nose. The young son was delighted. The father, when telling the story, recounted how he left the divider in place the following day but attempts by the pike to get to the minnow steadily decreased. By the third day the attempts had ceased altogether. The pike had learnt its lesson well – too well. It somehow understood that it was never going to be able to get from its side of the tank through to where the minnow swam contentedly. When the pike ceased all attempts to get from one side to the other, the father tried an experiment. He removed the glass divider from the tank and waited with bated breath. Despite the fact that the barrier was no longer in place, the pike continued to remain in its own half of the tank while the minnow stayed on its side. They never crossed over into each other's space. The pike – because it had repeatedly failed under previous conditions – now no longer believed that it could successfully achieve its aim. Past failure meant that it was no longer prepared to go on trying. How like us!

In our lives, we may also have received many disappointments and failures. The break-up of a relationship, the loss of a job, the crumbling of our sense of self-confidence, failures in study – any of these may have been a fact of life for us. If they have been, then the sense of being in a 'stuck' state may have a familiar ring about it. In the field of sporting endeavour, coaches often say that 'if you think you can, you can; and if you think you can't, you can't' – so in either case your thinking will be correct.

Anthony de Mello used to maintain that many of us have been programmed to fail. In fact he used to go so far as to say that we may not even want to succeed. When I initially heard this I thought the idea was cracked. Only a lunatic would believe that people would not want to be successful. Then I began to realise that it's not so much a case of people wanting to fail but rather that they do not try at all because the spectre of failure or defeat haunts them so much that inertia sets in. It's as if they are not prepared to set out in the race of life at all. In a sense, they defeat themselves. Put in religious terms, the 'Powers of Darkness' may have taken such a grip on them that coming into 'The Light' hardly seems possible.

In Gospel stories, we occasionally find Jesus encountering people who are affected just like those outlined above, who seem to be stuck. What Jesus did to counter this is what's interesting to me. He seemed to sense that a 'stuck' state is often associated with guilt and had a wonderful understanding that moving forward in such a state is not fun – it's scary. When individuals requested Him to assist them, He did. Even when friends of the afflicted put in a plea on their behalf, such pleas were often answered. Empowerment was granted. If we have the courage to ask with the same intensity for forward movement in our lives, perhaps the same grace will be granted to us.

*

EXERCISE ONE
Simple Awareness of Breath

The object here is to do just one thing at a time as completely and fully as you can. In this instance, you are attempting to concentrate on the inhalations and exhalations of your breath. Even your breathing can be a prayer. In the first lines of the Bible we are told that God breathed into man the first breath of life. In a sense we are imbued with life as we take each breath, even at night, when we are not conscious of it.

As usual, settle yourself in a quiet place and take up one of the usual postures for meditation. Different postures suit different people so test out the various methods in your spare time. You might favour a prayer stool, or lying on the ground, or sitting up western style on a straight-backed chair, or even squatting in a yoga-like fashion on the floor. As you start, try to be aware of your breathing. Think of nothing else. As you concentrate, you bring your attention back, time after time, to the activity you are engaged in. You may get distracted (in fact you almost certainly will) but do not despair. St Teresa of Avila is said to have told her novices that prayer time is made up mostly of distractions and you are also unlikely – unless you are very lucky – to be spared from wandering thoughts. If and when you notice those thoughts wandering, lead yourself gently back. Keep your whole being involved in the breath counting.

To keep the focus of your attention on your breath pattern, I find it helps to count internally as each breath goes in and out. This also seems to work for groups I operate with. As group members breathe slowly in, I ask them to count silently and slowly up to four. Then, when it comes to exhaling, I again ask them to make the same slow count, again from one to four. Just try this, 'Breathing slowly in, two, three, four – breathing slowly out, two, three, four'. This breathing pattern is repeated over and over again until a steady rhythm builds up which calms and settles you. Some teachers in the east suggest counting to much higher numbers and in Zen practice the usual time-beat seems to be to count up to ten, but for groups I have worked with a slow beat up to four seems to suffice and appears to work quite well.

Many people tell me, and indeed I find myself, that this exercise goes better with the eyes closed. That way you cut out distractions insofar as this is possible. You may occasionally find that some group members are reluctant or frightened to close their eyes. Often there is a reason for this, which they may wish to explore and delve into at a later time. For these individuals, ask them to almost close their eyes and let the tiny outline of the candle flame be their focus. I certainly wouldn't compel anybody to slavishly follow what is unhelpful or seems wrong for him or her just at this moment. Use the tools of the trade only if they help you.

*

EXERCISE TWO
The Healer
[Luke 6:17–19]

First read the text from St Luke's Gospel:

> And He came down with them, and stopped at a piece of level ground where there was a large gathering of His disciples, with a great crowd of people from all parts of Judea and Jerusalem and the coastal region of Tyre and Sidon who had come to hear Him and to be cured of their diseases. People tormented by unclean spirits were also cured, and everyone in the crowd was trying to touch Him because power came out of Him that cured them all.

St Ignatius of Loyola tried to encourage the practice of praying Gospel stories. Some of his methods are not particularly difficult and you can try them for yourself. You simply close your eyes and then let Jesus relive the narrative with you. In a sense the story is yours – your Gospel and your good news.

Begin as usual by sitting or lying still and, if you can, closing your eyes. You close the eyes so that sights or happenings around you may not be a major source of distraction. You are trying to form pictures or images in your head – or, as I would describe it, in your 'mind's eye' – of the event that the Gospel writers have described for us. When you close your eyes you may, hopefully, be able to see Jesus and be really there with Him. The incident described is not just a story from history. It's not just something that happened to a particular people in a designated place on a specified date. It's more universal than that. Christ came for all people. His mercy and love are as real for you or me today as they were for the people in the Gospel story.

As you sit and become quiet, try – in your imagination – to make your way into the story. It's as if you are in a cinema and the lights are going down. The curtains are drawn back and you are transported to a different milieu. Put yourself right in the action. Let the story unfold.

Picture yourself at the foot of a hill with a few others around you. Try to picture, by the amount of light available, how close to dawn it is. Some little distance away you can just make out the figure of Jesus as He kneels beside a rock. He has been at this location all night praying to His Father and news of His whereabouts has seeped out. In fact it came to you some little time ago. Let your mind ramble. Who told you about Jesus and where He was praying tonight? When did they tell you? Why did they tell you? What did they expect you to do with the news? If they hoped you would turn up at this place, what did they wish for you? Are they here with you now?

You might break off for a moment to pray especially in thanks for those who brought you to this place. In the Gospels Philip seemed to have a particular gift for bringing others to Christ. In our own lives, we may well have been gifted by a parent or relative who guided us towards the Divine. Pray for that individual now.

When you are ready, go back to the scene described. Remember it is early morning and Jesus has been at work all night. He has, we believe, been praying for us. Again pause for a moment. What might He have been praying about on my behalf? What particularly would I have liked Him to be pleading for? The Gospel passage tells us that many had come out that morning to beg for healing. Am I one of those? If so, what specific type of healing was I looking for? What difference might it make to my life if I received it?

Now allow the film in your mind to work its way forward. See Jesus as He begins to make His way down the mountainside. Does He look tired or distracted? Have others already begun to badger Him with their requests? Does the time look opportune to make your approach? Now He raises His head. He seems to sense that you are waiting for Him. More importantly, He seems to have a smile on His face and calls out your name as you approach. It appears as though He, even more than you, is grateful for this opportunity you both have for intimacy. Maybe that hasn't occurred to you before. Imagine what it must be like for Him to really want to communicate with you but to have very few opportunities presented to Him. As He rests His hands on your shoulders, His peace, love and healing seem to pour into your whole being. Notice how your spirit lifts, and pray that your soul may realise that something is changing within.

It states in the Gospel that those who went out of their way that morning to be near Jesus did so because they had confidence and faith that something good would be done for them. 'Lord, I believe. Help my unbelief'. Ask, with St Thomas, that your own fragile faith may be strengthened to believe that Christ's saving actions can also transform you. People have come today with very particular requests. Some were lame and others unseeing. They came because they were desperate and knew they needed something over and above what they could achieve on their own behalf. Am I similarly insightful? Do I know what I desperately seek and, even more importantly, do I truly believe that Jesus might go out of His way to give it to me? If the answer is yes, rejoice. If you are not so sure, then be with Doubting Thomas and ask that your faith might be strengthened.

In your imagination, watch as those in the Gospel story take their leave and depart from this place. They do not depart as they came, however. Their faith has allowed something miraculous to occur for a number of them. Try to spot those particular individuals as they make their way home. If your imagination is working you will hardly be able to miss them. Their very gait should give them away and if it doesn't, other clues will betray them. The fact that a horde of envious and curious bystanders surrounds them as they depart should alert you to the fact that something magnificent has happened for them.

Before you bring your meditation to its conclusion, take a few moments to reflect and be thankful for what you have experienced. If you were not sure what you needed to be healed, or if you are doubtful that Jesus was open to your request, ask that over the next few days the enormity of what you have been given may become apparent.

Conclude with an 'Our Father'.

Exercise Three
Who are You?

What's the most revealing or insightful response you could make to the question, 'Who are you?' Try this short exercise.

Begin, as people often do in the east, by concentrating on an awareness of your breath pattern. It's said that respiration acts as a bridge from the known to the unknown and I find that being aware of the pace and depth of my breathing brings a particular kind of stillness. Oftentimes, my mind doesn't want to stay in the present moment, which alone is real, but likes to wander to events of the past or to dreams of the future. In the east they are fond of saying that the art of living means that life can really only be lived in the present. Observing your breathing helps you to explore not only the reality of the body but also of the mind. As you slow down and your spirit begins to settle, some of the material buried in your unconscious may rise to the conscious level and manifest itself in various physical or mental ways.

Begin by finding a comfortable posture and settling yourself. Breathe in and out deeply and feel your whole upper body filling with air. I often find it helps to imagine that the room I am meditating in is filled with air, tinted with a colour I find relaxing. Draw the air in through the nostrils and imagine it making its way through your wind pipe and down towards your throat. Continue to visualise and see it moving down through your neck and into your shoulder area and thence down into your arms, slowly making its way to your fingers. As you slowly breathe in and out, imagine your chest area filling with the coloured fog. Watch, as the air you breathe in slowly begins to circle around your backbone and makes its way down to the pit of your stomach. Take a moment to place your hand over your belly-button and you should be able to feel the air as it arrives deep into the core of your belly.

Now put a finger on your pulse and count the beats. Become aware of the rate. Use your pulse frequency as a guide and breathe in and out slowly to the count of four. As you practise, you may notice that your rate of breath intake and output has slowed down. This is good. Hopefully the pace has decreased for a slower rate of inhaling and exhaling often produces a heightened mind-calming effect.

In the tranquillity, begin to mull over the question, 'Who am I?'

- What two words best describe me?
- What particular talents do I have at my disposal?
- How am I using my talents?

- How might I put these talents to better use in the future?
- Do I have a dream about what I might do over the next few years?
- If I do have such a dream, what am I doing to make it a reality?
- Are there aspects of myself that guide me or goad me towards the most productive me?
- If so, what are they?
- Do I have particular crosses to bear? What are they?
- Is there any possibility that I might transform these apparent crosses into blessings?
- How might I possibly do this?
- Now let me go back over my life to times when I felt things were cruel, hard, and unfair.
- Have there been trials or afflictions in my life that have helped me unearth strengths or purpose that I didn't really know I had?
- Are there aspects of my early family life that are impacting on my present performance?
- Is this impact for good or ill?
- Is there anything that others can see in me that I am not able to appropriate in myself?

When you are finished rest for a few moments in quiet and then thank God for any insights you may have gained.

Catching the Ox

CHAPTER 4

FINDING FOCUS

Not to know is bad; not to wish to know is worse
— African Proverb

The one important thing I have learned over the years is the difference between taking one's work seriously and taking one's self seriously. The first is imperative and the second is disastrous.
— Margot Fonteyn

Calamities in your life can bring growth and enlightenment. Being in the eye of the storm doesn't always have to lead to disaster. Anthony de Mello, during his workshops and retreats, was fond of pointing out that message. He would expound on the point by telling two stories.

The first concerns a wise man and his son, of whom the father was very proud. When his friends told him that he should always count his blessings and give thanks for how lucky he was, he had a stock answer ready for them. He used to tell them that a sensible person never took anything for granted or assumed good or bad would happen before an event actually occurred. You never really knows whether you are lucky or not until the story is finished for only the end result of a happening will really put things into perspective.

As if to illustrate this point, the servants of the wise man came running to him one day. They explained that his rather exuberant son had made off with a high-spirited horse for the day. Needless to say the lad had not asked for permission and, knowing how headstrong the youngster was, they predicted disaster. When the wise man was asked how he felt about his son's behaviour, he said, 'Maybe good, maybe bad – who knows'. Some time later the horse returned – but without its rider – and when the servants went to find out what had happened, they discovered that during the ride the boy had been thrown off and had broken his leg. The servants were full of misery and lamented how terrible the old man's luck was, but, true to form, the wise fellow repeated his usual mantra, 'maybe good, maybe bad, – who knows'. A few days later, some soldiers from the region came visiting the farm. As the country was preparing for war, they wanted to conscript any young men who might be residing on the farm. They were told that the son of the family was indeed present but was upstairs in bed because his leg was broken. As soon as the soldiers checked this fact out and found that it was true, they moved on, grumbling that a broken-up adolescent was of little use to them. The wise old man, on hearing the news, said to his servants, 'Now you can see how difficult it is to know whether events will ultimately turn out to be good or bad. Often it takes time before we know whether what has befallen us is a blessing or a curse'.

To illustrate the point further, de Mello used to tell this second story from the east. It concerned a bird which sheltered each day in the withered branches of a tree that stood in the very centre of a vast deserted plain. One day, a whirlwind uprooted the tree, forcing the poor bird to fly hundreds of miles in search of new shelter. Finally, after a long search, it came to a forest containing many fruit-laden trees. The moral of the story, as Anthony de Mello explained, is that you cannot always tell when disasters might in fact be paths towards new opportunities. If the withered tree had survived, nothing would have induced the bird to give up its comfort and security. The apparent catastrophe was really, for the bird, the catalyst that impelled it towards future progress.

In our own lives, it is often very difficult to judge whether events that befall us are likely to bring afflictions or possibilities of growth. St Ignatius suggested that the best way of finding out whether such events spring from a good or evil spirit is to take time out for ourselves occasionally to review what has been going on. Soren Kierkegaard, the Danish philosopher, suggested something similar when he said, 'Life can only be understood backwards'. This, unfortunately, may cause something of a problem, as most lives have to be lived in a forward direction and we thus have to artificially create ways of checking how our personal relationship with God is progressing, not to mention devising systems that can judge whether the trials that befall us stem from healthy or noxious sources. At all times we have to try to see what lies beneath the action. Does it have more meaning than is at first apparent? If we can gauge what effect a particular event is having on our interior being, we are half way towards knowing whether to be perturbed or not. It can be beneficial if we have some sort of a system in place that asks questions effectively of us about where good fruit or grace is occurring in our lives. As we grapple with this task it's easy to settle on the wrong questions, or even to ask the right question but for the wrong reasons. Human frailty tempts us to have deaf ears or an unseeing eye or an uncaring heart when 'home truths' loom on the horizon.

For any of this self-revelatory material to appear it is usually necessary for a certain amount of 'time out' or 'reflection time' to be created and most religious orders have tried to follow this practice for years. They make an annual retreat, during which they try to look within. Members strive – at least in theory – to become aware of their own vulnerability and examine areas of failure in their lives as well as zones of success. They try to see where they have been damaged, why they have been wounded, and who has being involved in the breakage.

As you might imagine, people vary with regard to the amount of success they have with this task though most admit that it does help to develop a certain skill in self-noticing. You need to ask, 'What's going on in general, and what's going on in me?' What effect are events, experiences, personal conversations and the like having on me and what moods are being triggered because of these experiences? During the retreats a sort of template or mind map is created covering the areas of head, heart, gut and soul and it's highly profitable to tune in to these feelings if you are a seeker after self-truth. Notice also what's going on in your body for our bodies act as a Geiger counter, relaying information about what effect the different situations we find ourselves in are having on our contentment and health. It's as if something deep within us is trying to relay how life experiences are affecting us. As we try to build a healthy relationship with God, the ability to listen carefully to our own wounded story can be revealing.

Material that rises to the surface can offer a sort of 'wake up' call if we allow it to, for each item that reveals itself has some significance. Mulling over the experiences and the effect they are having may help to clarify 'hunches', but this only happens when we stay vigilant. If what comes to the surface startles you, it might be to your ultimate advantage for you may find yourself compelled to do something about it.

By taking the time out to mull over what is going on internally, we are sometimes struck by the realisation that if we want recovery or wholeness we may have to change our behaviour. We begin to notice wounds, some of which we thought were healed, but now, as we look at them more carefully, we sense that they can be ignored no longer. Cuts or crevices, which we imagined had successfully knitted, may well show themselves to have flared up again. They have become re-infected. Vulnerabilities are exposed, and vulnerabilities are a painful reality.

I recently came across an idea that might be useful to those struggling along the path of self-discovery: it was suggested that the seeker after truth might create for himself or herself a sort of 'impact journal'. I would describe such a journal as a notebook or ledger where you write down what you notice about internal 'spirit' activity. Start by examining the head, heart, gut and soul areas of your being. While going over the past few months of your life, you might ask yourself what 'patterns' are presenting themselves. Do these patterns bring growth or decay? Are they destructive or pressing the wrong buttons within you? What might these 'wrong buttons' be? Why are they causing you grief? Why are they cajoling you to act in a harmful way towards yourself? What's going on within you that's interfering with your self truth-seeker's role? These questions may help you re-visit and tend to your wounded places.

Having looked at ourselves and found out what's going on within, we might be brave enough to turn outwards. Have a look at the type of culture you live in and try to ascertain what effect that culture is having upon you and your faith. Is it helping or hindering your progress towards God? Most sociological books will tell you that the pace of change within society or culture has escalated dramatically in recent years. To comprehend the change and to try to gauge its impact on your lifestyle and values, just go back 20 years and think what life was like then. You didn't have computers on every desk, or mobile phones, or satellite televisions in every home. 'Lap-tops' were an unheard-of innovation and paid part-time work for school-going students was not something that many engaged in. The way we lived had a definite structure. Authority resided fairly clearly in certain individuals and institutions. It seems to me that family rules and regulations were – by and large – fairly unambiguous.

Parents' authority may have been questioned or objected to but the fact that such authority existed, and was expected to exist, was more or less the norm. School structures and parish life were also well defined. Those in authority laid out the rules and felt confident about doing so. Those being led were clear what was being asked of them and understood well enough when they were overstepping the mark.

Now move your mind forward and think of today. A new 'do as you like' philosophy seems to have appeared and puts intolerable strain on all concerned. Without accepted guides or guidelines, people take it upon themselves to act as they think fit. This is wonderful up to a point. It gives a sense of freedom. It helps an individual to feel they are in charge of their own destiny. However, it also has a down side. Being your own judge and jury can lead to confusion of the worst type. It can mean that we are like the student who asked his master, 'Can you give me a sign to know when I have become enlightened'. The master's reply was terse: 'You will find yourself asking, "is it myself who is crazy or is it everyone else?"'

In this new society, old certainties disappear. Without maps or guidelines, a new task is placed before us. Self-examination becomes more important than ever. New skills are called for. Watching your body and how it reacts to what it is going through provides an assistance of sorts. Everything from your 'life journey' is recorded in your body. Emotional pain can manifest itself in highly surprising ways: your shoulders may sag, your neck may have a pain in it, and your energy may become choked and sluggish. Any or all of this may happen at such a leisurely pace that it can be extremely difficult to notice what is going on. In our prayer, we can ask some searching questions. Is God giving me crosses to bear? Might it be at all possible to turn the cross I have been given into a gift or blessing? Can I recall a time in my life when experiences seemed hard, cruel, or unfair? Are afflictions that have befallen me destructive and damaging or – on closer inspection – might it be possible to unearth gold from these difficulties that is not readily apparent at first sight? Regarding life within my family – are there aspects of that life that are impacting negatively upon me?

Let your mind wander over experiences or situations that have happened to you during the last few months. Let them act as teachers. Is it possible that we might have had a life-changing experience but missed its meaning? Remember that Socrates said that the unexamined life is not worth living and it's partly for that reason that we mull over, and jot down notes on, the experiences we go through. One of the reasons for keeping a journal is that it helps us appreciate both the experience and its possible meaning. Reflecting on what is happening to me, and why it is happening, as well as noting the effects that the experience has had on me may well change the way I react to similar situations in the future. In the east they say that if your sight is poor it's important to realise that you need glasses. If your hearing is impaired, you'll miss what others are saying. If your view of the world is jaundiced, your reactions to what happens to you will similarly be flawed. Most of us, as the African proverb puts it, think our own mother is the greatest cook in the world. We are hardly likely to see our own world-view as biased. To get better perspective, we might listen to the comments and insights of those around us. Don't be too insular. Pick up wisdom from any source that presents itself to you. We don't want to be like a missionary who visited a retreat centre to speak about the places and peoples he had encountered. After he departed, one of his listeners went to the director of the centre and asked whether travel broadened the mind. The director, who had been forced to live with the preacher at the retreat centre while he gave his address, replied that in this case the experiences talked about seemed only to have spread the preacher's narrow-mindedness over a wider area.

It's possible that even the most earth-shattering encounters may pass an unawake person by and leave little imprint. Developing a sense of acute awareness is never easy. The world-famous astronaut, John Glenn, relates how this fact came home to him during the space exploration programme he had to go through. Candidates for the programme were asked about themselves during the initial stages of selection. They had to give 20 answers to the question, 'Who am I?' Not many managed the task successfully. Glenn said replies to the question were bright and cheerful at first. Answers were given, but they nearly always zoned in on status, achievements, or what positions people had managed to attain. As contestants tried to delve down within themselves and find out who they were at their core, they struggled. So will we. Knowing our truest and deepest selves is not easy.

Anthony de Mello tried to provide meditations and fantasy exercises to help us with the task. They provide a sort of self-knowledge periscope that assists us in pinpointing the cause of our changing moods. One of the benefits of meditation is that it assists the one meditating to be clearer, more focused and more able to handle how he or she does feel, even if these feelings are painful or confused. It provides the possibility of integration – of being more in touch with your deepest self and where God might reach you. The fantasy prayer practices, which de Mello was so fond of, contain a certain wisdom we may not realise. At times they help us mull over aspects of our life which we would find incredibly difficult to do if we had to face the issues head on without the assistance of imagination. Cardinal Basil Hume understood very well. He believed that God does not always do His talking to us during times of prayer but that sometimes gets His message across to us outside that formal prayer period. By this I think He means that the effort we invest during prayer time somehow produces the possibility of sudden flashes of self-knowledge, but these insights may only occur after we have finished the formal prayer.

Fantasy prayer exercises we engage in may gently skirt around questions such as:

- What is my calling in life?'
- Am I living that calling?
- Perhaps I have rejected the calling?
- What is it that I really seek?
- What am I most proud of in my life?
- Who or what have I forsaken?
- Do I know why I have forsaken these principles or individuals?
- What do I value most in life?
- Where does my power come from?
- How and when do I use my power?
- Do I honestly want to change anything about my life or myself?
- What would it take for me to change?

Really difficult questions like the above, if faced head on, would be brutally hard to undertake. The beauty of the fantasy prayer exercise is that it allows such challenges to come to the surface of our consciousness without scaring us away. We can use the fantasy exercises to explore personal questions that otherwise might be too threatening. If we want to know what it is about us that infuriates others we might approach the question by means of a fantasy exercise. When we jot down our discoveries, notes may help us decide which rough edges we need to smooth.

In his book, *The Screwtape Letters*, C. S. Lewis initiates a dialogue between a senior devil and his junior colleague. He wants to show how the devil is constantly manipulating affairs so that the worst side of human nature is brought into play. All sorts of stratagems are used and outlined; the individual being worked on generally cannot see what is happening because of being too close to the action. It's with this scene in mind that we keep our 'impact' journal for jotting down daily occurrences which may show up the wiles of the devil.

Such introspection was strongly favoured by St Ignatius, the founder of the Jesuits, who regularly looked into his own life and interior moods and suggested that his followers should do likewise. At some level we are a mystery to ourselves and the better we manage to unravel that mystery the more likely we are to remove blockages that hinder our interaction with God. St Ignatius, to facilitate the constant checking of his conscience, examined his behaviour on a daily basis and kept an eye on how different actions of his impinged on his inner feelings. He hinted that his followers would be well advised to chew over feelings, emotions, reactions and moods that they find themselves experiencing. Do this at very regular intervals, he counselled, because if you delay you allow blind spots to build up and distort the truth.

In the locker-room of our memories we all carry a suitcase full of individual memories and emotional baggage. Our task during moments of prayerful reflection is to prise open the rusted locks of that suitcase and rummage around inside. People are reluctant to do this for two reasons: first, because it hurts and second, because it takes time. We feel disinclined to undertake this task and our reluctance is understandable. Somewhere, deep down, we sense that painful home truths may rise to the surface which will have to be owned, understood and then dealt with. Not only that, but the hard work and introspection sometimes appear to have been hardly worth the effort. The rewards may seem puny. If we are expecting instant insights they may not occur. At times the wisdom given does not make itself apparent – at least, not initially, and not when expected. They may only come into focus outside the time of prayer, as for example, during the quiet time of an annual retreat. In that oasis of solitude, a person may be given inklings of where growth has been occurring and where it is likely to show up in the future.

One of Christ's gifts to us was that He helped us imagine ways forward which were fresh and invigorating. He left people in a better state than He found them. Jesus was unique in this regard.

It would appear that some of the meaning attached to our experiences can be gleaned as the actual events are taking place, but other wisdom will only be seen clearly in retrospect. Sometimes the world seems to be moving so quickly that we cannot digest all the data that is coming at us. Occasionally, a mirror is needed to reflect the meaning of events that befall us. Friends, work-mates and companions can, by their comments, be that mirror. Nobody grows alone. Dialogue of some sort is needed. Dialogue with others, yourself or God is essential. The independent observations given by others may be the key to understanding our own trends and patterns. By their choice of words, their body language, their eyes, they will send out their message. By paying attention to these clues, your self-awareness will be increased. During our early training as Jesuit novices, we used to have sessions where our confrères were given the opportunity to point out which habits of ours drove them mad. It was painful but profitable for almost all. Only one student I can think of proved to be the exception. Of him it was said, 'He takes correction well – but not seriously'. Little chance of change there!

*

EXERCISE ONE
Starting Out

Go to your quiet space and seat yourself. Ensure you have a straight-backed chair in position and use calming background music if you find that helpful. If you are working with a group, check the music out beforehand to ensure that it is not jarring or unsettling. Before beginning the meditation, use one of the preparatory exercises given earlier. Focus on your breathing, your posture, or how each part of your body is feeling. If you skip this early, quietening down phase, it is likely that you will neither settle satisfactorily nor become absorbed in the meditation and you should not be too surprised by this.

If and when distractions begin to occur, form a picture in your imagination. Imagine a jam-jar full of water in front of you filled with coloured counters. Think of these counters as your distractions. Still working with your imagination, tip the jar over on its side and watch the distractions flow out from the vessel, all the while telling yourself that your distractions are quietly flowing away. Now you are almost ready to begin.

I've said that one of the best ways to commence with a meditation session is to begin with a breathing exercise. Remembering to breathe and noticing your breath rhythm might seem like a very odd instruction. However, in the east they teach that your breath is your greatest friend. They start there because they know that a settled breath technique brings with it a relaxed demeanour. Some instructors say that focusing on your breathing is the only technique you need to lead you into meditation and while this notion may be a little too simplistic, it has a grain of truth about it. A steady flow of air in and out does bring with it interior composure.

As you breathe in, feel the cool air as it touches your nostrils and makes its way down to the core of your being. As you breathe out, keep your attention on the air coming back up through your whole being. Notice any changes in the quantity and quality of your breathing style.

Sometimes our breath may be short or shallow – at other times long and deep. Your job during this beginners' exercise is to observe your breathing pattern without attempting to alter its pace or rhythm. As you engage in this practice, you may notice your thoughts wandering. If distractions seem to be invading at every turn, gently put them away by reverting to an awareness of breath. Don't force anything but each time you feel yourself drifting off into a sea of distractions, lead you thoughts gently back to the breath.

Sometimes it helps to give yourself a running commentary as you try this exercise. Speak to yourself at your breathing pace and say, 'Now I'm breathing in, now I'm breathing out'. After a while you may notice that your pace of breath slows down somewhat.

Certainly if you are engaged in meditation over a weekend's workshop, the change of pace is quite discernible. Everything seems to slow down. After a little practice, your awareness of your breathing pattern may become more obvious to you. You can do this exercise quite often during the day. If you suddenly feel distressed or irritated, you might try to allow your eyes to close briefly and focus on your thoughts. It is surprising how even unpleasant emotions can be dispersed quite quickly if you allow them to be released by the breath. After about ten minutes, bring this exercise to its conclusion.

*

EXERCISE TWO
A Pilgrimage Walk

Almost every day we have experiences, meetings and encounters with others, often followed by dreams at night. Some of these dreams and experiences pass by almost unnoticed while others have quite the opposite effect – they leave an indelible mark. It might be fair to say that much of what happens to us falls somewhat between those two extremes – it's neither riveting nor completely forgettable. If we take the time to mull over the real happenings, not to mention the dreams, they can often be a treasure-trove of revelation. They can even be material for meditation.

Let me give an example. Very recently, a small group of friends and I undertook a pilgrimage to northern Spain. Our task was to walk the ancient pilgrim route to Santiago de Compostela. Others who treaded the path with us gave us their company on most days. Almost all had a tale to tell or a dream to share. Numbers of our fellow walkers carried with them what I can only describe as 'dream journals' – little notebooks into which they recorded their dreams each day. By this method they felt they were making a commitment to know themselves better. When they took some of the material gathered in these journals and used it as matter for meditation, they found the results were often quite illuminating.

Our companions were not shy about handing out little pointers and hints about how we might best utilise such a journal and you may find their comments helpful if you would like to try the exercise yourself. We all know that dreams have a habit of fading from our consciousness very quickly so keep a pen and paper by your bedside and, as soon as you wake up, spend a few minutes quietly in bed with your eyes closed remembering what you can. Then open your eyes and commit what you have remembered to paper. Recall the imagery, sequence, characters and setting insofar as you can and jot everything down. Some fellow companions on the walk with us said they gave their dreams a title – it often proved useful and revealing at a later date. Offer yourself a refresher course too by going over the material a week or so after you have jotted the points down. See if you can notice any patterns, repetitions or issues that bring distress. Your notebook will, in a sense, help you to hold a mirror up to yourself in order to spot your 'shadow' self at work.

What does this 'shadow' self look like and what does it do? In what situations or with what people is it most likely to appear? When is it most uncontrollable? Does it tend to team up with any other trait within you to wreck havoc? These questions will help you understand what fuels the best and worst parts of that 'shadow' self. Work with the 'shadow' self – not in opposition to it – and eventually the best you will emerge.

Working with our dreams is not the only way of increasing self-knowledge and self-understanding. On the pilgrimage, we found that sharing deep conversations also helped. To initiate such conversations, strangers usually asked each other where they were from and why they had begun the hike at all. On our second day an elderly gentleman who looked unlikely to complete the pilgrimage joined us. As well as being old and frail he looked tired. Something burned within him, however, and as he broke open his story the purpose of his walk became apparent. About a year earlier his wife had died of cancer. This devastated him and – as he said himself – he began to sink into himself. Friends and family tried to lift the gloom but without success. Finally one old nun suggested that he might like to take on something worthwhile in his wife's memory. Slowly the idea of raising money to research ways of combating the wife's particular form of cancer began to formulate itself in his mind. He became enthusiastic and started to make plans. When his friends saw that he was seriously considering taking on a pilgrimage walk which would take him not less than a month to complete they became gravely concerned and tried at every turn to block his progress. The old man would not be deterred, however, because he now had a purpose to drive him on. When we met him he was more than two-thirds of the way through his dream. He had also collected a considerable sum of money towards research into his wife's illness.

So calm yourself now and begin to settle. Take in steady breaths of fresh air and draw them right down to the pit of your stomach. Next let the stale air escape from within you as you breathe out and watch as the dullness begins to lift. Be aware of the natural rhythm of your breathing as it makes its way inwards and outwards. Notice whether your body would be a bit more comfortable if you stretched a little or yawned, and, if so, give it that latitude.

Picture yourself on a pilgrimage walk like the one I have described above. You know you still have hours to walk before nightfall and the old man I have mentioned has fallen into step beside you. He begins to tell you about his life, his marriage, the death of his wife, and his steady slide into listlessness. Have you ever been in that sort of a black hole yourself? The old man tells you how his friends and family cajoled him into getting back up off his knees. One of them gave him a direction and an aspiration when he hadn't the energy or ebullience to motivate himself. Pray that if you find yourself similarly downcast, your friends may be just as energetic and effective on your behalf.

*

EXERCISE THREE
A Reconciliation Service Based on Nature

For this exercise, sit quietly and keep your head upright. Straighten your back and bring yourself to quietness by slowly breathing in and out to a steady beat. Place one hand on your abdomen to feel your deep inward breath as it makes its way down to the pit of your stomach. Inhale through your nose and exhale through your mouth, making a quiet whooshing sound like the wind as you gently let the air out. Stay relaxed and focus on the sound of your breathing as you slowly become more and more relaxed.

Now imagine yourself in some beautiful place out of doors. Nature itself has a lot to teach us and plants and animals often provide useful hints towards God's presence as well as His love because, just like us, they need to feel the rays of God's sunlight as it caresses them. At this moment, I may need to allow God's love caress me in order to experience His generosity in my life.

As I begin the exercise, I begin to walk around the chosen place and note the various objects of nature as I encounter them.

First, I may spot some ivy. See how it manages to take root in the most unlikely of places and clings to whatever is available. I pause for a moment to ask myself if I similarly cling to old securities or other people instead of stepping confidently out into the future?

Next I may spot a squirrel. It hoards away much of what it finds. Do I, in a similar manner, store up hurts from the past instead of letting them go? Do I hang on to the sour taste of bitterness, not wanting to let it go lest I forget the one who I allowed deposit such feelings within me?

As I walk on, in my imagination I may come across a thistle. At first glance it's garnished with beautiful purple flowers and green leaves but it has also got its prickles. Am I a bit like the thistle myself – soft and vulnerable on the inside but presenting a spiky exterior to the world? How hard do others find me to deal with when I allow myself to display a shell of that hue? What kind of forgiveness would it require of me to blunt those prickles? Who exactly would I need to forgive in order to make the thorns less sharp?

Next to come into view may be a dandelion. It's bright and friendly on the outside but its insides taste sour and poisonous. Can I be a bit cold and poisonous myself and uncaring in my attitudes to others?

In nature's garden, good and bad mix together continuously. It won't be long before nettles raise their ugly heads. Known chiefly for their sting I ask myself whether I sting as well by means of sarcasm, anger or intolerance?

I now lift my gaze up from the ground. Overhead, birds glide to and fro. I notice a magpie with its beautiful, piebald colouring but the pleasure is diminished by the constant chatter, chatter, chatter of noise that is emitted from its mouth. It never shuts up. Am I a bit like this myself, making a great deal of sound? Do I like to chatter and gossip? Has my loose talk hurt others and damaged their character?

Close by, a starling makes its presence felt. You can hear it almost before you see it. Other birds are wary of it and give it a wide berth. They know from bitter experience that it seldom brings rest or contentment to those around it. Do I spend most of my time talking without listening? In a prayer context, do I pour forth a continuous stream of prayers while never allowing Jesus to speak to my heart?

Two last birds may come into view. The pheasant may stroll around if the season is right. Proud as punch, head cocked in the air, seemingly unaware of any danger.

As a final entrant, a robin may appear. It stays in its own patch, singular and alone. Am I possessive of people, or do I keep close control of my own ministry, making it a no-go area to others who might want to help? Finish by offering a prayer of thanks for the gorgeous gifts of nature around you.

*

Exercise Four
'Andrew Figures'

Settle yourself comfortably, eyes closed, and try to still your mind. You may help yourself to settle by imaging that as you draw the breath into your body, you are drawing the Spirit of God inside yourself. This should give you inspiration.

It sometimes helps to make the experience more real if you count to yourself as you breathe if. Say interiorly, 'Now I breathe in, two, three, four and now I breathe out, two, three, four'. Alternatively, you might say quietly to yourself, 'Breathing Christ in, breathing worry out', or again, 'Breathing goodness in', and hold that inward breath gently for four or five seconds, before saying 'breathing worry out' as you let go of all the stale air inside your body.

As you undertake this exercise, be aware of the air streaming in through your nostrils, filling up your lungs and then be conscious of that same air – with its healing calmness having done its job, departing from you through your lips. If you try this exercise for a little while it will help you to focus awareness only on your breathing.

After some time working on this breathing exercise, you will hopefully begin to notice that your breathing has slowed down a good deal more than heretofore. On retreats and weekend workshops, I notice that participants find their breathing does begin to change its pace – it becomes more even and slow which results in a more relaxed and peaceful frame of mind. You have now prepared the ground for the fantasy exercise ahead and in your own time you move into it.

During the pilgrimage walk to Santiago de Compostela, pilgrims prayed each day as they walked along. I don't know about others but I found I often prayed about the life stories of fellow pilgrims as they related these along the way. One young woman pilgrim came from a town in Germany that has a beautiful cathedral. Much to our surprise, she had never been inside it. In fact she had not been to any sort of chapel in years. In her youth, her parents had a habit of telling her precisely what she should do in her life. As she grew older, she found this practice more and more irksome. Anything they told her – including the benefits of having a faith life that nourished you – she dismissed. She kept far away from chapels, temples or shrines of all sorts. 'So what,' I asked, 'has brought you to something like a pilgrimage experience?'

'A friend,' she said, 'who could see I wasn't happy about a relationship I was in and who was concerned enough to suggest I should take time out by myself to discover what I wanted from life. She is a Christian, and I know she often prayed, and I thought I would try it out for myself – so here I am.'

We might take time out to ponder on people like this unnamed friend. I call them 'Andrew figures'. Among Christ's disciples, Andrew seemed to have a special ability to point others towards Christ and then step back into the shadows himself. By looking back over my own life, I may become aware of people who pointed me in a positive direction at different and difficult times. As I call them to mind, I spend a little time praying in thanks to and for them.

If you are undertaking this prayer exercise in a group you might ask members to take a sheet of paper and note down any 'Andrew figures' they can call to mind. Sometimes it helps group members to share with – and listen to – others in the group insofar as they feel able.

*

EXERCISE FIVE
Christ Lost in the Temple

You will find it easy, if you are leading a group in prayer, to use any Gospel story if you know the scene well yourself and have an overall sense of where the narrative is leading. Go slowly. Let each sentence of the story make its mark. As the saga unfolds, images are presented. Allow time for those images to form in the minds of group members. In each Gospel story, Jesus is the figure we often want to keep our attention on and the smart group leader normally attempts to relate the Gospel stories in the present tense so that the story may have its full impact. They also leave time at the end so that participants can take time out to be with Jesus. Allow that time. Don't be stingy.

As a general rule it helps to remember that there are different parts to a well-worked Gospel meditation. Firstly, take up a helpful posture, whether it be sitting, kneeling, or lying down.

Next, bring the group to quietness (or attempt to!) by means of one of the preparatory exercises. The one I usually use, as you may have noticed, is observing your breath pattern. You can, however, equally well use one of the other awareness exercises I have scattered throughout the book.

The third element is describing the scene and/or incident. By means of concise storytelling, the listener sees, hears, touches and feels the events as they develop and unfold. You – as narrator – need to encourage group members to feel that they are really present at the event being described. It may be a consolation to know that the Lord will be with you as you set about your task.

Finally, a period of time is left at the end of the Gospel story so that the listener can be with Jesus and try to realise the gifts they have been given. They need time to give thanks, to ask for help where that is appropriate.

Now open your Bible and search out the story of Christ's childhood appearance in the temple. Read the story over carefully for yourself and see what points you think emerge from it that group members might find helpful to think about.

*

Exercise Six
The Cemetery

During meditation, the window to the unconscious is often opened up a little and we get a peek at what is going on below the surface – items we have repressed or pushed down. Some describe these moments as being a little like watching the movements of a swan as it makes its way across a lake. Above the surface, things seem to glide along with little or no effort. Below the waterline, however, a furious thrashing about may be going on. At times the subject matter that appears during or after the meditation may take the form of symbols or stories or images. If we think about the material that emerges, it can often explain much of the otherwise inexplicable events that are going on for us. We can get a better handle on why we are depressed, obsessive, destructive or evasive or just frozen in fear by certain situations we encounter.

So go now and find yourself a suitable place for prayer – perhaps a spot you have made holy because you have used it on previous occasion for prayer. Make sure you feel safe and secure in this location and then settle yourself and try to become still. This may not be easy. Modern life dictates that we live at a pace many find unhelpful for reflective living.

Still we do the best we can to achieve tranquillity.

First try to become aware of the way you breathe. Build up a slow and rhythmic breathing pattern and allow this settled breathing to give you a sense of repose. This may take time. Remember that muddy waters – if they are allowed become still – slowly begin to clear. Your task at this moment is to open up this clarity by achieving a sense of deep inner wisdom insofar as you can. Draw each breath deep into your body, picturing each breath in your imagination as it makes its way down to the base of your stomach. As you breathe in you may be helped by slowly and silently counting off each breath in the following manner, 'breathing slowly in, two, three, four ... breathing slowly out, two, three, four', and see if the interior counting has the effect of grounding and settling you. I find the simple task of counting off each inward and outward breath silently to myself keeps my mind focused but this may only be because my mind tends to jump widely from place to place unless it is kept under tight rein. When you feel this exercise in breath awareness has slowed and settled you, begin the next part of the operation. Start imaginatively to sketch in the scene that I outline below.

What I would like you to imagine is that you are attending the funeral of a close friend. In fact you are making your way behind the hearse to the graveyard. There are various ways of doing this. One way that might help is to visualise the happening as if it were an event captured on video. As you watch the events unfolding on video, you notice that you yourself are up there on screen and are part of the action. Another way of getting into the meditation 'space' is to envisage yourself as an artist, sketching the scene for posterity.

As soon as you have a reasonably clear picture of the event in your imagination, allow your mind to formulate an image of your dead friend. Remember his or her gifts and talents. Recall how they were often placed at your disposal. Now spend a little time considering what a pity it would be if these talents came to a sudden full stop. In a sense, how futile your friend's life would have been if everything ended here.

Now let your mind travel onwards to the scene described in the Gospel story of Lazarus. You think a little about Lazarus and how his friends and family must have been devastated by his demise. The sense of hope they possessed through knowing and loving him has been rudely torn away. Keep your gaze fixed on his sisters. Their words to Jesus show they are shattered. Even his sister Mary, normally so tranquil and benign, is finding it difficult to keep the anger and sense of injustice out of her voice. In your imagination, roll the video on a little and listen for the

words of Jesus. Hear him ask the sisters, 'Do you believe that your brother will rise again?' The question seems – at first sight – unnecessarily
brutal. Jesus is asking for a lot here. Not the 'soft soap' approach for Him.
Not even smooth or consoling words.

At this point we might remember Christ's own death and dying. We
may be given an image of Christ Himself in His own tomb. We might
remember that Christ was adamant that death – His own particularly –
was not the end of affairs. As St Paul stressed, without the Resurrection
there would be no point believing in Jesus. The tomb acts as a sort of
chamber leading towards greater glory. We know that Jesus Himself has
already trod these paths and shown the way towards fuller life. He has
revealed glimpses of glories to come through His own post-resurrection
appearances and these can act as a spur to us to progress onwards with
buoyancy and hope.

Finish by praying the 'Our Father' so that you might have a little of
that confidence and expectation for yourself.

*

EXERCISE SEVEN
The Struggler

I am a chaplain in a university and, as already mentioned, a few of us
decided to go on a pilgrimage walk abroad with some of the students. As
you trudge along, you make plenty of time for yourself to reflect on what
has been going on within you. You can hardly avoid doing so because
not only do you have time but you also meet all sorts of fellow pilgrimage
walkers along the way. Their stories bring new light to your own hidden,
and hitherto confused, reflections.

One couple we continually met along the way left a deep impact
upon me. One of the pair was healthy and walked with vim and vigour,
but the other had obviously felt the strain of some of the more difficult
sections of the hike and walked with great difficulty. Most days, they
started out before us but we passed them at a good pace after a few hours
and I seriously doubted whether the one who had trouble walking would
ever reach the end of the hike. The usual practice is that individuals
stop for rest along the way so that's what we did. Invariably, the same
couple would catch up with us as soon as we sat down and each evening,
when we reached our day's destination, we would find that they would
also have reached their objective. It might take them longer, and I'm

sure the healthier one must at times have been frustrated, but they always reached a safe haven by nightfall. I dedicate this meditation to all
who have to hobble along as they journey.

Let us begin. Go to a safe place for prayer and close your eyes. Give
yourself a moment to settle and then feel the tension slipping away. Try
to notice the style and pace of your breathing and let yourself become
aware of each breath as you inhale and exhale. At this point allow your
mind to recall one of the Gospel stories about healing. The one that
comes to mind – and the one that I used as I walked the pilgrimage route
in the company of the above couple – was Christ affecting a cure for the
man with the withered hand from St Luke's Gospel, chapter 6, verses
6–12:

> Now on another Sabbath He went into the synagogue and began to teach,
> and a man was present, and his right hand was withered. The scribes and the
> Pharisees were watching Him to see if He would cure somebody on the Sab-
> bath, hoping to find something to charge Him with. But He knew their
> thoughts; and He said to the man with the withered hand, 'Get up and stand
> out in the middle.' And he came forward and stood there. Then Jesus said to
> them, 'I put it to you; is it permitted on the Sabbath to do good, or to do evil;
> to save life, or to destroy it?' Then He looked round at them all and said to
> the man, 'Stretch out your hand.' He did so, and his hand was restored. But
> they were furious and began to discuss the best way of dealing with Jesus.

Take your time and visualise the story as best you can, sketching in the
scenery as best you can. What does the scene look like and how many
people are around to witness the event? In your imagination, you are at
the place of the miracle yourself and you might begin by focusing your
attention on the sickly person. He must have got himself noticed by
Jesus. How did he do this? Next watch how Jesus asks him to step out
from the rest of the crowd and show himself. Do you think the man was
embarrassed by having to show his infirmity? How much did stepping
out in front of the crowd cost him? You might break off for a moment
here to look at yourself in the scene. You will probably appear like all the
other onlookers – fairly anonymous – with no very obvious injuries but
the reality may be somewhat different. Which one of us can say with
truthfulness that we are completely whole? So what is dead in you? Try
to stay for a few moments (or even a little longer) with what happenings
have caused a withering within you. It may be that you have recently
undergone a trial or some kind, or someone close to you may be ill or
dying. Your job or home circumstances may be slowly whittling your
energy away even without you being fully conscious of the fact.

As I walked along the pilgrimage route, I became aware that dead leaves and flowers were being slowly taken back by the earth where they gave nourishment and vitality to new life. Perhaps the elements that have died within you recently have potential. In your imagination, place those elements on the ground and realise that they may have life-giving properties. Be aware of death turning into new life. For that to happen, some action may be needed on our part. Return your gaze to the man with the withered hand and note how Christ presents an opportunity to him. Watch his response as he steps forward.

If something is being asked of me can I step forward too? Often we are paralysed with fear at the prospect of such a challenge. Pharisees of all shapes and sizes may well try to block our progress. Pray for the faith not to let any hindrances get in the way of your progress.

CHAPTER 5

WHEN MY FOCUS IS BLURRED

It is not the answer that enlightens, but the question
— Ancient Proverb

While in India I heard this story about a young woman who had the good fortune to live at the time of the Buddha. When her first-born child was about a year old, it fell ill and died. Grief-stricken, the poor woman began wandering the streets with her baby in her arms, begging anyone she met for medicine that would restore her child to life. Most of the people she came across were embarrassed and tried to keep out of her way. Some even thought she was mad and actually laughed at her. Finally, she came across a wise and kind old man who told her that the only person in the world who could perform the miracle she wanted was the Buddha. She went to him and laid the body of her child at his feet, telling him her story. The Buddha listened with infinite compassion and then said gently: 'There is only one way to heal your afflictions. Go down to the city and bring me back a mustard seed from any house that has not been touched by tragedy.' The bereaved mother searched high and low in every house she could find for she was most grateful that she finally been given a way out of her pain. Search as she might, however, she could not come across an abode that fulfilled the conditions laid down. She visited house after house, but everywhere she inquired, some form of affliction had touched the inhabitants. Deaths or misfortune had occurred in all the establishments. Finally she realised that the Buddha's condition could not be fulfilled so she took the body of her child to the burial ground and said goodbye to him for the last time before returning to the Buddha. When he asked if she had brought back the mustard seed, she answered that she was beginning to understand the lesson that he had been trying to teach her. Grief had made her blind and she had thought that she was the only one who suffered at the hands of death. 'Why then,' asked the Buddha, 'have you come back to me?'

Leading the Ox

'To ask you to teach me the truths,' she replied, 'of what death is, what might lie behind and beyond death, and what in me, if anything, will not die.' The Buddha told her that there is only one law in the universe that never changes, namely that all things change. Everything is impermanent. He explained that the death of her child had helped the young woman to see that life is an ocean of change, and that change sometimes includes unbearable suffering.

Sogyal Rinpoche in his book, *The Tibetan Book of Living and Dying*, says that death is always hard to face but he has heard of many cases of people who were diagnosed as terminally ill but refused to be beaten by the news. They withdrew a little from life, sought out solitude and truly faced themselves, as well as the fact that they might die, and subsequently were healed. They clearly looked at the issues facing them and managed to convince themselves that if the worst happened, they could cope with it. This may well have happened for the artist, Rembrandt, whose wife died while he was still young. It seems that after her death, he entered a period of profound depression and his art suffered. Eventually, he bounced back and began to believe that life could go on despite his difficulties. As he regained his good spirits he began painting with new power, passion and purpose. Some critics think that the act of accepting his wife's death was a turning point in his career for it raised him to a new artistic level.

Elisabeth Kubler-Ross, one of the foremost writers about the effects of bereavement also has words of wisdom about the way we need to change our focus if serious situations befall us in our lives. She says that she knew a good deal about the theory of how people have to change if they encounter really difficult personal situations but it was not until she suffered a stroke herself that she found the message hitting home. A short time after her stroke she found herself overcome with feelings of anger – a stage she has described so graphically in her book, *Death and Dying*. She noted with some wit that 75 per cent of her friends seemed to evaporate while she was in her 'anger' phase because they couldn't handle her rages and she wasn't afraid to point this out in her writings. Others with a literary bent have also noted the reactions of those around them when personal change is required, though not all are willing to write about it. Recently, a journalist friend of mine went to visit his aged and infirm father who he had not seen for quite some time. At first the conversation between the two was almost non-existent but, after a while, a kind of thaw set in and words began to flow, even if these words were rather serious in nature and centred on the family's history. The old man started to tell tales that seemed like dim and distant memories to the younger man. These included events from the early days of the parents' marriage. My friend really started to perk up and pay close attention when stories about his mother surfaced and a number of revelations emerged. These were stories the journalist had never heard before. When he asked why this colourful family history had never been hitherto revealed, the father answered, 'You're an author and we all know about authors. I was afraid that anything I told you would be written down and blathered around the neighbourhood. I didn't want you to make a holy show of our whole family.'

Anthony de Mello would have been delighted if he had heard that tale for he constantly used stories to illustrate the points he was trying to make and many of his stories belonged to his own personal history. He would have been a dangerous man to have as a friend for he kept an acute eye on what went on around him and learned lessons from everything he saw. One of his Jesuit companions used to boast that he had been a priest for 50 years and had never once missed his daily hour's meditation. I'm sure he expected lavish praise. I would have expected that myself. That wasn't what he got from Anthony however, who pointed out that such behaviour was not in itself worth praising or something to be proud of. 'It's what you do with your prayer and what effect it has on your behaviour that is important,' he pointed out.

At times the lifestyle we lead and the behaviour we get up to has to be put down to conditioning or programming from our family history or even from our culture. It takes honesty to admit that behavioural traits may have been learned by rote. Ask yourself, 'Has my lifestyle or my faith beliefs been dictated to me by patterns laid down years ago by my parents or school?' This happens more regularly than we might like to think. De Mello mentioned time and again that in his therapy groups he came across individuals who weren't acting as themselves or out of their own honestly held beliefs or values. They were dancing to somebody else's tune. Put simply, they didn't know who they really were at their core. Those looking from the outside could see shades of the individual's mother or father but the fact that they were mirror images of their parents wasn't apparent to the individuals themselves at all. They were strangely ambivalent about who their true inner selves really were or what they believed in passionately.

In honest prayer, the real inner person will at some stage come to the surface. This will happen as we ask whether our actions or words are coming from sincerely held beliefs or not. The ideology that drives us may be part of an overall package handed down by our parents, our school or our religious order. If that's the case, we may begin to realise that we are like puppets on a string, dictated to by authority figures of yesteryear. We like to think that we act independently but there probably isn't a gesture, an attitude, a thought or a belief that hasn't been greatly influenced by those who went before us.

To spot this factor within ourselves, we need to be self-observant and watchful and by this I do not mean that we have to become totally self-absorbed for that only means that a person is concerned and worried only about himself or herself and this is neither healthy nor wise. Self-observation, on the other hand, is a method by which you watch everything you get up to insofar as this is possible. You observe as if the episode were happening to somebody else. For this to work, you need, as it were, to step back a pace or two and get things into perspective. You watch your actions as if they had no connection with yourself whatsoever. In this way you see what effect they are having on you. Such detachment may help you realise that your anxiety, fright or depression is more detrimental to you than you had supposed because you have identified overmuch with it.

A number of saints, when talking about prayer, encourage us to notice both rapturous and forlorn inner feelings for they are pointers as to how God is working within us. They know that the soul is where the inner and outer worlds meet. St Ignatius of Loyola, in his book *Spiritual Exercises*, illustrated how he believed God is actively at work in the world and in our hearts and presumed God is present and active in each one of us. By looking over our daily affairs and noting prayerfully what is happening to us, he believed we might find out where we have been meeting God or possibly where we have been trying to avoid such a meeting.

Our minds are divided into two parts – the conscious and the subconscious – and we want now, if we can, to look at both sections. First, concentrate on the conscious mind. It is mostly adult, rational, aware, awake, transient and thinking. Go to it first to seek signs of God's at work. Try to spot where the Lord may have been lurking in your recent history. If you can use your conscious mind to discover where He has been operative, that is excellent. However, if such scrutiny is proving rather ineffectual, try other strategies. This is where our subconscious comes into play for the subconscious mind tends to be emotional, irrational and dreamlike, with a tendency towards concealment. It can be primitive, chaotic, and illogical but also a little like the proverbial elephant that never forgets. Given the opportunity, it may well throw up memories and remembrances that – on a conscious level – would be extremely difficult, if not impossible, for you to handle. During our fantasy work, hidden meanings sometimes float to the surface and begin to become intelligible and comprehensible. At times they need to be untangled, because fantasy – by its very nature – is protective and shields us from having to grapple with the harsh realities of life. That is just as well, for many of us would be devastated if we tried to face the realities of life head-on and unaided.

To see how fantasy can be helpful, let's try an exercise. Seat yourself in a comfortable position and pay attention to your breathing. Follow your breath as it enters and leaves your body. As you breathe in, notice how the muscles tighten in your chest and, as you exhale, let those muscles relax. Do this for a dozen breaths or so. Now take note of how you are feeling mentally, emotionally, and physically. Try to image that you are a divided self. One part of you feels as you would ideally like to feel at the moment, while the other – perhaps a better barometer of your present state of being – may be more fatigued and less inspired than you would wish it to be. As you inhale and exhale, take a few minutes to notice the gap that exists between where you are – and where you would like to be. Bring before your conscious imagination someone who is important to you and begin a dialogue with him or her. First go over the particular gifts this person has bestowed on you. Is there any area of yourself they have helped you understand more clearly? Next go on to dialogue with your work and look at the interaction between yourself and your labours. Is the work you do trying to tell you anything? As you begin the dialogue, you may start to realise that certain elements of your work energise and empower you. Now initiate a dialogue with your body. It may have been a stranger to you for too long and you now need to get together to check whether you and it have been fair to each other. Ask gently, and your body may respond with honesty. Are parts of you in pain or in a state of complaint and if so, which parts are hurting and what are the hurting parts trying to tell you?

Next I move on to thinking about my dreams. Initially this can be quite difficult for I may either forget the contents of recent dreams or find that they all seem to blend into one and become a bit of a blur. No logical pattern may be discernable. If, however, I bring my memory back into order, important trends may begin to materialise and start to float to the surface. Don't be put off if at first things seem blurred and hazy. What the subconscious is throwing up can be vague and nebulous. The revelations can also be difficult to embrace. Past memories, which come to the surface, may have been less than pleasant and, if that's the case, it is likely that we will want to block out or refuse some of the information that seems to be coming our way. It may seem easier to move around the grief and head directly for areas of healing. Certainly that is likely to be our first temptation but such a course of action is unlikely to be productive. Fantasy is a useful tool because it can help us to go through – rather than around – our difficulties and in this way a degree of health is restored. In today's culture it is noticeable that many do not choose this path. They try to bury pain and hurt and to this end they use drugs, alcohol, television, physical activity or over-work. They hope these activities will sweep their inner distress under the carpet but most honest practitioners know only too well that this doesn't happen. If anything, the pain slowly but surely gets worse. Keep an eye out here for another factor that may be acting as a brake to your progress in prayer. Despite its unpopularity today, the reality may have to be faced that exterior forces may be at work. For centuries, masters of Christian spirituality have spoken about the wiles of Satan at work in the world and warned us to be on our guard. They liken this force to a bully – belligerent, but weak. If left unchallenged, it creates mayhem, but if faced and confronted, it tends to flee. Attempting to face the darkness, however, or even trying to understand what it might be about can be a wearisome business. Most don't even want to begin.

Those who are slow to confront evil, or who are unwilling to help themselves in any way, don't fare too well in the Gospels. St Augustine noticed this and said that it seemed to him that their actions stymied Jesus and appeared to block His goodness and grace. This was not because of any weakness within Jesus but because those unreachable persons refused to open a door to Him. An oriental proverb says that pearls do not lie on the seashore and that if you desire one, you have to dive for it. Similarly, if you want to grow spiritually, you need to leave a door at least partially ajar if you want good things to happen.

De Mello often enlivened his audience by telling them about a nitpicking individual who never facilitated his own spiritual progress and who complained incessantly to God because he never seemed to have any luck in life. His last grumble was his finest: 'God, why don't you give me a break and let me win the lottery?' He was surprised by God's reply: 'Why don't you give me a break yourself? Why don't you buy a ticket?'

Personal growth comes with a price tag. That fee may include personal experiences of a painful variety. For many of us when this happens, we shut up shop. We don't want to pay the price. We run away. Deep down we know that catastrophic events leave aches that are almost unbearable so we choose to sidestep the ache and make our way directly towards the healing. It doesn't work. A wound not allowed to heal consumes from the inside. If we could but bear them, such painful experiences would cast illumination into dark corners of our being and reveal areas where growth has not yet occurred. In the quietness and the pain it's conceivable that we may be able to pinpoint areas of unhealthy attachment. These areas are like strings. They tie us down rather than free us.

Recently, on a workshop weekend, a participant highlighted this point when he shared a recurrent dream he had been having about loss of freedom. He dreamt he had a white dove tightly clasped to his chest, which he held on to with all his might, and he wondered what the dream might mean. No one knew. The workshop group did, however, offer a suggestion. Next time he had that dream, they suggested, he should open his arms which held on to the bird, and see what happened. That's exactly what he did, and it cost him, for in the dream, as soon as he opened his arms, the bird sprang free. It did not, however, fly away. It gently circled his head and then returned quietly to perch on his shoulder. It also uttered just one sentence: 'Now, at last, we can both be free'. If we can cut the strings of our unhealthy attachments, perhaps we can attain the same freedom.

*

Exercise One
Finding Forgiveness

As you begin the meditation make sure that your body is comfortably positioned whether you are seated or lying down. Check that you have enough space around you to prevent feeling hemmed in or inhibited. Begin, when you feel ready, to breathe rhythmically in and out, reflecting the rhythm of the universe. You usually do this unconsciously, but at times of increased stress – for example, when coming up to examinations – it becomes quite difficult. Recently, at exactly such a time, I offered a series of meditation evenings to university students and many felt so 'stressed out' that they could hardly manage to obtain inner quiet or a peaceful rhythm of breathing at all.

Try to maintain a steady, constant, relaxed, rhythmic breath pattern for yourself as many teachers in the east maintain that – when it comes to meditation – your breath is your greatest friend. In fantasy exercises what floats to the surface sometimes surprises us but you must let this happen in its own time and in its own way. Trying to force material to the surface is usually unproductive. We can neither dictate the subject matter nor the timing of inner revelations and maybe that is just as well. It's as if we had an inner censor for our own safety, which allows the challenging material out in its own way and time, and so prevents us from being overwhelmed with too much too soon.

Now build up a picture in your head of some safe, favourite spot of yours that exists in reality or is a figment of your imagination. Place yourself in this spot and visualise someone coming toward you who you know, have been hurt by, or are not very keen on. When you are ready, move towards the disliked person and offer a symbol of love, peace and forgiveness. This will probably not be easy but as you present your gift, try to be aware of how the other person feels. Do they keep eye contact? If they speak, what do they say? Now you take the initiative and make eye contact with them. Salute them as a fellow traveller in life and acknowledge that it is often those we find it difficult to resonate with who teach us most about ourselves. If their presence has provided revelations, thank them. When you are ready, allow the picture you have built up in your imagination to fade, and come back to the present time and place. As you once more focus your attention on your breathing, gently bring the meditation to a close.

*

Exercise Two
The Wedding Feast at Cana

Seat yourself and begin the meditation by undertaking a 'sounds' exercise. Do this by relaxing your breathing and first listening for any sounds you can hear outside the room. Go slowly for you may be able to distinguish between quite a number of competing noises. Without rushing, slowly bring your awareness into the room you are working in and notice any movements going on there. Perhaps you can single out music playing in the background, or a clock ticking, or the tiny sound of breathing coming from others who are with you. Be aware of how you are and check the points of contact between your body and the chair. Relax any tightness as you breathe outwards and, on each 'in' breath, notice the cool air as it makes its way through your nostrils. When you feel a sense of quiet and stillness, allow yourself to enter into the following scene taken from chapter 4, verse 2–6 of St Mark's Gospel:

A wedding is taking place. You have been invited. Look around.

What's the setting like? Are many people present? Are you a special guest seated close to the bride and groom, or a distant relative positioned well away from the main action? Let your eyes sweep around the room and notice the great earthen jars close by – the type normally used at weddings from 100 BC to AD 200. Just stay with those jars for a moment.

Now comes the difficult part. Use your imagination to picture yourself as one of those jars and notice the unique features of your own design. First, you might realise that you were created for a particular task. Your business is to hold things. Liquids. Perhaps your surface is less pristine than you would like it to be, with minor imperfections and scratches. Are these blemishes preventing you completing the task you were designed for? Think about yourself in relation to the other jars that surround you. All of you are at this wedding feast and you have already noticed that Christ, who is also at the wedding, has made use of some of the others. Now it's your turn. You can hear Jesus telling the waiters to bring you over. Jesus touched the other casks and made them special. Do you want Him to touch you? Before you are presented to the wedding guests, does anything about you need to be changed? If so, what? Take a little time to wonder what change you might ask Jesus to effect upon you. Ask for that change. After some little time return – in your imagination – to being a human being again and thank Jesus for the blessing He has given you. Slowly bring your meditation to a close.

*

EXERCISE THREE
Bringing your Sickness to Jesus

Find a suitable spot for prayer and use a breathing exercise to get you into the right frame of mind. When you are ready, imagine an ordinary day in Jesus' life. We are told in the Gospels that on many occasions Jesus preached all day and by evening found himself faced with dozens of infirm and distressed people looking for his attention. In this meditation I want to place myself among those sick ones. All day, I imagine that I have been waiting in line, outside Peter's house because word has gone around that Jesus is in the neighbourhood. I have been crippled all my life and have heard about others, similarly afflicted, who had great things done for them. So many people in our locality had been speaking about Jesus and how power flowed through Him that I want to take my chances. Today, as I wait in line, I am acutely conscious of all these others around me on a similar mission to myself – we are all looking for a cure. We're certainly a motley-looking bunch but I don't expect that will put Jesus off. I look inside Peter's house and catch a glimpse of Him and at exactly that moment He peeks out and sees us – a gang of 'down-and-outs' – and for a moment I fear He will remain where He is. Now the door of Peter's house opens and Jesus comes out. I'm the first one He spots and so it's in my direction He first comes. Others move closer trying to catch His eye but my moment has come and I'm not going to let it go. I plead with my eyes. He is in front of me now, looking down, seeing my crooked leg. He begins to apply his hands to the crippled me. Something is happening. I can feel power coming into me. My leg begins to straighten. Soon it is strong enough to put my weight on. As I begin to stand I can hear the words of Jesus beginning to penetrate my darkness. He is asking me to come with Him, to help Him. I begin to tell him I have been damaged all my life. A bit of a failure really. I can hear Him say that this does not matter. He can use both my talents and me. My heart is singing. I am walking again. Jesus is asking me to do something with and for Him. He first healed me but now He is asking me to heal others and He seems to be suggesting that if only I believe in myself, then I too can empower others as well as myself. As I stretch out my hands I can feel the healing power of Jesus flowing through me. I close my eyes and with my whole heart I pray. I have only just been healed myself but now I am been asked to be a co-redeemer. I ask a blessing on the people beside me. Something is happening. The sick ones beside me are beginning to respond. Their hope and faith seems to draw out something within me I didn't know I had. Before my very eyes I begin to see them change and prosper. Those around begin to look upon me as if I were a healer myself. Perhaps, with God's help, I am.

Finish the meditation by thanking God for his goodness towards you and ask that you may have the courage to take up any gifts that He may be offering you.

*

EXERCISE FOUR
Come and See

First read this story from chapter 2 of St John's Gospel:

One day two of the disciples were in John the Baptist's company when suddenly Jesus passed quite close by their group. When the two friends asked who this new arrival was, John the Baptist told them that they should go to Him and ask. The two began to follow Jesus and asked, 'Rabbi, where are you staying?' 'Come and see,' was His only response.

Now begin your prayer. At first things may not be as perfect as you would like, but persevere. As you inhale, try to relax and be at peace with yourself. Become aware of any noise outside the room where you are praying and try to distinguish the different sounds you can make out. Use this awareness of sound to build an aura of peace around yourself before bringing your attention inwards to focus on sounds within the room. Finally, bring your attention deep within yourself and try to see if you can notice the very tiny sound of your own breath as it enters your body. You may begin to become aware of the slight coolness of the air on the tip of your nose as it is drawn deep down into your being.

Now build up the Gospel story in your mind, as if it were a movie being played inside your head. You are with one of your closest companions. For months now you have been in the company of John the Baptist because he seemed to bring a sense of purpose to your life. Now the day of reckoning has come. Christ has appeared, but whether that will make a difference in your life or not is unclear. A gift is being offered, but does not have to be accepted. Firstly, notice the appearance of Jesus. He comes into the picture slowly. Only John seems to notice the significance at first. Something or someone however, prompts you to ask about the stranger. What prompted you? Now you are told to go over and check Him over for yourself. Not an easy task and one, perhaps, that might embarrass you. Gather up the courage you need to approach Christ and when He offers His invitation make sure you have the audacity to take Him up on His offer. You will need to let go of what is tried and tested. Loosen your grip from the hand of John the Baptist. This will not be easy because he has been a good guide and teacher. Your journey will take on new challenges and new directions. The beginning may not be easy. The end is as yet completely unknown. When will your journey end? Will you find what you are looking for? Do you even know what you are looking for? Now finish the meditation and relax.

*

Exercise Five
She has Chosen the Better Part

Sit or lie down and pay attention to your breathing. Follow your breath as it enters and leaves your body and as you inhale, ask that energy may be given to you. As you exhale, let your muscles relax. Continue with these deep and slow breaths for a couple of minutes. Concentrate on what is happening while you breathe and watch particularly for the cool air as it comes into your nostrils and the slighter warmer feel as it makes its way out again. Whenever your mind wanders, take note of the wandering and then return to an awareness of your breath before you begin.

I start by trying to sketch a portrait of the two sisters, Martha and Mary, in my mind. They have vastly different temperaments and personalities – one driven, the other slightly dreamy. I imagine the two sisters as Jesus comes to their house on this special day. What have they been up to? Martha is the one I concentrate on first, as she is the one who comes to the door. Jesus can spot her fine qualities straight away – solid, conscientious, a Trojan worker, and house-proud. I'm sure Jesus would have wanted to compliment her on her work, but He also wished her to seize her opportunities when they presented themselves.

So now, Lord, I begin to think of the times when I was similarly preoccupied and didn't notice Your knock. For the times when I mumbled and grumbled and felt that work was being unfairly dumped on me.

Then I move on to the second sister, Mary. I watch her just sitting there, talking about the bits and bobs of her life and wishing that she could find even more time for reflection and leisure. As I sit here watching the scene, I ponder the words of Jesus, 'She has chosen the better part', and I take a few moments for myself during which I put my hopes and fears for the future in His hands.

*

Exercise Six
The Tree

Sit comfortably in a chair and place your feet solidly on the floor. Now begin to notice the breaths you inhale and exhale from your body. As you breathe in, tell yourself silently that you want to breathe in peace. On each out breath, remind yourself that you are exhaling inner tension and disquiet. Remind yourself of any items in your life that may be causing you disturbance and let those elements go, insofar as you can. Use your imagination and visualise a relaxed state taking you over within. Feel tension evaporating. Allow the steady pace of the breathing work its own magic. It might be worth remembering that meditation has been used successfully in many cultures and over many centuries to prevent high blood pressure and other forms of stress. With regular practice you can learn to live more and more in the present moment.

So now be still and begin to picture this scene in your imagination. Imagine yourself as a tree situated somewhere in a natural setting and try to ascertain what type of a tree you are. Are you big or small, bushy or scraggy? Do you think that you are tall or short, grand or rather plain? Note where you have been planted – in rich soil that nourishes, or barren landscape that has to improvise? Do you survive on your own, or are there a host of other trees in the proximity? If there are others, are they of the same variety as you or different? Do you live your life quietly without communicating with them or do you regularly discuss how things are going with those around you? Begin to look at your roots. How healthy are they? Note the spot they are planted in and see how they stretch into the soil. Do they find the earth nourishing? What in fact sustains them? Do they feel deprived of any particular source of nourishment?

As a tree, you live through different seasons so try to imagine yourself first in autumn. Feel your leaves drying up and changing colour. Get in touch with any feeling you may experience in your leaves and branches. As your leaves begin to fall off, do you feel naked and vulnerable or in the early stages of new growth?

Now autumn gives way to winter. Have the chills of this season killed off all the good things that surrounded you or have they thankfully removed elements in the environment that were unhelpful to you?

The seasons are changing in your mind and now winter is over and spring is making its entry. Notice the soft showers that bring with them fresh water for your roots, along with a gentle climate which encourages new growth. See and feel the buds within you growing and bursting forth. What is growing within you?

Now move on to summer, you have optimum conditions to encourage maximum growth. How are you making use of these conditions and how much growth is taking place?

When you feel ready take a few moments to become a person again and become aware of your surroundings. Try to get in touch with the experience you have been through and see what similarities and differences there are there between your life as a tree and your daily life as a person. Is there anything about yourself or your situation that you particularly like or dislike? Anything you would like to change? Take a few moments to relax and then end the exercise.

CHAPTER 6

DISCERNMENT

It is much harder to judge yourself than to judge others. If you succeed in judging yourself, it's because you are truly a wise man
— Antoine de Saint-Exupéry

The Far East is a great place for stories. One I like concerns a ruler who needed to make a trip to a foreign land. Before he went, he looked around his apartment and noticed his pet bird in the corner, for he kept it in a cage. He asked this bird if there was anything it required before he departed and it pleaded, 'Free me.'

'No, that I won't do,' the ruler replied.

'Well at least let my cousins know how I am when you meet them on your travels abroad.'

After some time the master reached his destination and met the birds in question. As requested, he relayed the message he had been asked to deliver. Upon hearing that their cousin was caged, the foreign birds immediately fell down in a faint. When the man got home he related what had happened to his pet. Straight away the caged bird keeled over in its cage. The master, thinking it was dead, opened the cage to examine it, whereupon it flew away, singing with joy because now it was free.

Before flying off altogether, the bird said: 'The message you delivered – disaster in your eyes – was in fact good news for me. I was given an insight, for I realised that the way to obtain my freedom was being explained to me by you, my captor.'

That's the essence of this chapter. Learn to distinguish good from evil and do this by means of the experiences life offers you. Jesus Himself had to discern. He faced many 'crossroad' points in His life. Remember how, in the Garden of Gethsemane, He faced a nightmare situation. It seems clear that He had some premonition of the disaster about to befall Him. Many have wondered whether He could have chosen to avoid the catastrophe that lay ahead or whether He simply had to follow His destiny. The Gospels do not give us a definite answer. They hint that there

Coming Home on the Ox's Back

was a plan, but whether the following-out of that plan was inevitable or not is left unclear. It's not unusual for honest and thoughtful Christians to question aloud whether God has a life blueprint for each one of us. If this is the case, they wonder whether the plan has to be followed or not?

Down through the centuries, gallons of blood have been shed over this question of predestination. To try to come to some understanding of whether God does have a personal plan for each one of us, we might begin by looking at the life of Christ Himself. He can teach us about discernment. It may be easier, however, to look at a contemporary figure like Henri Nouwen. Many will be familiar with this modern-day mystic who has written much about his life, his struggles and the way he tried to follow God's will. He talks often and at length of how he reached some of the more difficult decisions in his life. In his fine book, *The Road to Daybreak*, he focuses on one particularly dark period of his life. At the time, Nouwen was lecturing at Yale Divinity School and things were not going as he would have liked or expected. His teaching, and his life in general, were both causing him anguish. This seemed strange to him as he was in a prestigious college and was both known and respected. He should have been happy, but deep down he knew he wasn't. That was the starting point. He had reflected on his life and knew that things were out of focus – at least in his mind.

Because he is both thoughtful and honest in his writings, Nouwen illuminates something about personal discernment. He first goes over the facts. He had visited South America on a number of occasions and these travels had set in motion a disturbing thought. Possibly Christ was calling him to live and work among the poor of Bolivia or Peru? Back home after these travels, he reflected upon this possibility and certain doubts began to intrude. He looked at hard facts in the cold light of day. He knew that his spirit was at times brittle and realised he wasn't capable of being a missionary in a Spanish-speaking country.

Upon further reflection, he noticed something else which didn't please him but which he knew to be true. The grinding struggle for fairness and equality, which he witnessed on a daily basis during his visits to Latin America left him discouraged and despondent. Just living there left him feeling flat and his inner calmness deserted him. This shocked him. Not only had he noticed this himself but also stray comments or hints from his friends began to ring in his ears. These hints suggested to Nouwen that he could do more for the people of Latin America by his writings and lectures than he ever could by living amongst them. These facts were not easy to digest. Still it was clear to him that idealism, good intentions and a burning heart for the interests of the poor did not in themselves constitute a vocation to living and working among the marginalised.

The process outlined above were Nouwen's steps to discernment. He had clarified the situation for himself. He now knew that taking on a mission in South America would bring him nothing but heartache and for the call to such a mission to be authentic, he first had to be called – and then sent. His quiet reflection had convinced him that the natives of South America had not, in fact, summoned him. Nor, indeed, did the Christian community appear to wish to send him on such a mission. He had been through a process of self-discernment and gathered information along the way. This process had unearthed a certain unease regarding his current lifestyle. Some type of change seemed necessary. But had he got the qualities that such a change might demand? Honesty and wisdom persuaded him that he was not cut out for the apostolate he had in mind. His body or mind would not take easily to the constraints which living among the poor of South America would demand. Wisely he decided to remain for the moment where he was. He believed that the next judicious step forward would be shown to him. It was, but not at a time or place of his choosing.

The sense of unease, which had plagued him heretofore, continued. When he tried to put his finger on why this was so, insights came. The students he worked with in the university neither wished nor asked for what he had to offer. He was keen on getting across to them some of the burning issues of South America, but, if he was honest with himself, he knew that was not their interest. They needed something much more basic and, in his judgement, what they needed was more than his particular specialisation could provide. This left him feeling discouraged and dissatisfied, for, in his own words, 'I found myself sulky and complaining'. He knew he felt slightly rejected. Correctly or incorrectly, he felt unvalued and unloved by both his university faculty and students. Whether these feelings were true or false was immaterial. They were his and that made them true for him. God was speaking. The signs were clear. He would have to go on with the discernment process about how his life should proceed.

Around that very time, something strange happened. A visitor turned up at his door unexpectedly and the encounter left him feeling uneasy and uncertain. This visitor came with personal greetings from the famous Canadian, Jean Vanier, who was inviting him – out of the blue – to become part of a L'Arche community for the mentally handicapped. In effect he was offering Nouwen a new home and a new beginning. Those were the simple, cold facts. Trying to make sense of them was a more complicated proposition. A move such as the one being suggested would uproot him completely. What the world held dear – a secure home and a solid reputation – would be undermined. People would question both his wisdom and his sanity if he accepted such an offer. It did occur to him vaguely that perhaps this is the very way God offers us opportunities. As Henri Nouwen turned these issues over in his head and heart, he realised that what he was being given was exactly what he always asked for. He had always hoped that God would give him a sign of how best to proceed. Where should he go? Where would he be most useful? Now, in a way, his prayer was being answered. A welcoming hand was being extended in his direction and what he had asked for he was now receiving. The only problem was this: – now that a path forward was manifesting itself, he found himself reluctant to accept it.

Nouwen's story illustrates many of the uncertainties we may face when trying to ascertain God's will and plan. A path presents itself, but it may be poorly defined. In our terms, it may be badly lit. The journey being suggested may have to be undertaken in the dark. Confusion, fear, and loneliness may be part of the package. In order to 'map' a sensible route for any undertaking that may face us, Nouwen gives some tips. He says that he felt he was guided. Something like an inner voice kept speaking to him as he tried to discern what would be best for him. This inner voice hinted that it might be worth using his gifts as a writer and resume a routine he had practised in the past, keeping a journal.

In the diary, he noted what went on in his prayer life and what suggested itself to him as he listened to his inner heart. In the journal, he recorded what happened to him day by day for he wanted to discern the Lord's plan for him and knew that an honest periodical that gave flesh to his inner longings and questions would be invaluable. You might think it easy to keep such an inner journal but it's not. Nouwen happened to be particularly good at it. His jottings highlighted for him the fact that he felt an intense desire to preach the Gospel, but some instinct told him to hang back. Now was not the time for such active work. His gut feelings told him that now he needed to take time out. He needed to pray, to meditate, to read, to be quiet, to sit still with an open heart and an eagle eye. If he did this, God would show him what the most positive way forward for him might be.

As he saw it, two rival voices seemed to be competing with one another for his attention. The outer voice kept saying that he could do much good here and now at the university. The inner voice, however, had a different message. It wondered whether it was wise for him to remain where he was. Staying there seemed to bring feelings of flatness and misery. In such a state, how could he minister to others? Was it wise to try to lift the spirits of others while risking the possibility of losing his own soul? His feelings of being rejected, of sensing inner desolation, were clear signs, in his mind, that he wasn't following God's intended path for him.

Nouwen understood only too well that the fruits of God's Spirit are generally not sadness, loneliness and separation. He also knew that if he were prepared to take a gamble on the opportunity being presented to him, he had a method for testing out the rightness and wisdom of his decision. If this opportunity were coming from God and were followed faithfully, it would bring with joy, peace-of-mind, serenity and a sense of community. These may be useful yardsticks to hold on to.

If God has a plan for us, and if we remain true to that plan, equanimity should follow. Often, however, it's not easy to determine the rudiments of any such plan. St Ignatius had a 'trick' which might help us here. He maintained in his writings that it is extremely difficult to see the rightness or stupidity of a deed at the very moment a decision has to be taken. He suggested that it is simpler to see the best route forward if we take the time to look backward first. Let me explain.

Take time out occasionally to cast a glance over how things have been for you in recent months. This might be done on a yearly retreat or on a quiet weekend away. Such times can be very illuminating. They provide breathing-space to step back and get things into perspective. I've often been struck by how difficult it is to make out what exact direction I am travelling in as I stand in the bow of a boat in open sea. I have no clear reference points. I have no markers or guidelines. On the other hand, if I stand in the stern and looks backwards during the journey, I can make out much more easily where I have come from just by looking at the trail left in the water.

So it is in our lives. By looking backwards we can ascertain where fruit has been harvested – what actions, people, events, and situations, have brought unexpected rewards. This knowledge guides us towards the next positive step forward. Try it. Go over the past few months you have lived through. Replay them. Try to be as honest as possible. In retrospect, mull over the events that have brought you real, lasting, beneficial fruit and you may be very surprised by what you learn. Happenings, which at the time they occurred you felt were very beneficial for you, may now seem very trite. As you replay them in your mind, they may show themselves to have been a good deal less valuable than you had originally supposed. Conversely, experiences and practices that appeared rather trivial when you first engaged in them, may now, in retrospect, assume much greater significance.

St Ignatius is reported to have said that wise individuals do not judge the wisdom or otherwise of an action at the moment they have to perform it but rather by looking back afterwards and checking what fruit has been produced. Trying to judge the wisdom of an action at the time decisions have to be made is never easy. Let's take a tiny example. One event which I eagerly await each year is the English soccer cup final. It's marked down in my diary from the very beginning of the year. Normally a gang of us gets together and watches the proceedings on television. The group always looks forward with anticipation. We should know better. The event regularly turns out to be a damp squib. When the great day dawns, we park ourselves in front of a television set. Hour after hour, bits and pieces of soccer snippets are relayed to us. We learn about the team's preparation, profiles of the players, their wives and their families, and thence on to how they actually progressed to the final. Next we are brought on to the team coach as it makes its way to the ground and we even go with the players as they have their pre-match lunch. After this the team warm-ups are shown, and final tit-bits of news are relayed with religious intensity. At last, the great moment arrives and the match begins. By this stage each member of our group has already watched hours of television and looks a bit like a zombie. The final itself is such a prestigious event that players are nervous and the match is often a rather boring affair. Added to this, if no definite result is reached by the end of normal time, an extra half-hour is played. By now, we have been watching television for five hours or so. Most of us are in a stupor. Suffice to say that I regularly find myself with a headache that evening. It's about the only evening in the year when I do have a headache.

On the opposite end of the scale, I regularly try to go hill-walking at weekends. In fact, most Sundays when not otherwise engaged, I take to the hills with a similarly minded group. Often the weather looks most unpromising before we set out and I have serious doubts about whether I should go or not. However, past experience has taught me that I virtually never return from hill walking – whatever kind of weather is thrown at us – without being mighty pleased that I made the effort. What looked like it might be a bleak and gloomy prospect if weather forecasts were to be believed, nearly always delivers a great deal. These two examples show that some experiences – while promising much – deliver little. Others, seemingly without potential, actually yield a good return on our investment. With this knowledge we can decide where to place our efforts in the future.

*

EXERCISE ONE
The Potter

First read the text from chapter 18, verses 3–4 of the Book of Jeremiah:

> So I went down to the potter's house: and there he was, working at the wheel. But the vessel he was making came out wrong, as may happen with clay when a potter is at work. So he began again and shaped it into another vessel, as he thought fit.

Sit or lie down in a quiet place and pay attention to your breathing. Follow the breath as it enters and leaves your body. As you exhale, let your muscles relax. Do this for a dozen breaths or so. Now become aware of how you are feeling mentally as well as emotionally and physically at this moment. Imagine two selves within you, one feeling as you would ideally like to feel while the other – perhaps more representative of your state of mind – may be more tired and less inspired than you would wish it to be.

When you are ready, begin to formulate a picture in your head. Imagine a potter sitting at his wheel, the clay ready beside him. He scoops up some of the clay and begins to work. For minutes, then hours, he works with that clay, moulding it this way and that, trying to create the perfect shape he has in mind. Sometimes the clay is not as moist as he might wish. At other times it is less malleable than he expected. The clay seems to resist him occasionally but still he carries on with his task. Finally, something beautiful emerges and he sits back to look at his creation.

Now imagine that God is the potter and you are the clay. Think of the times when you were less open to God's influence than you wished to be and thwarted as well as mangled His design. Yet still He persevered, as He has constantly done with you and me.

Finish by giving thanks for His constancy and goodness and ask that He may not give up on His task.

*

Exercise Two
Bringing your Pain to Jesus

Sit or lie in a comfortable position and leave your arms down by your side and your legs uncrossed. Now breathe in deeply and draw the breath down into your abdomen. As you inhale, count slowly and silently 'One, two, three, four'. Then exhale slowly, again counting up to four in your own mind. Continue to breathe in and out, matching the breaths with your interior count. Notice your breathing gradually slowing and be aware of your body as it relaxes and your mind becomes calm.

Now imagine that Jesus is close beside you and speaking some words from scripture. He is reminding you about the passage where we are told to forget about making any offering if we have not yet let go of old resentments and bitterness. Let your mind think about those who have hurt you and settle on any one person whom you feel did you a wrong or whom you are afraid of, or one you dislike or find difficult to relate to. Perhaps you can let your mind focus on a person you have difficulty forgiving. Holding this person in the palm of your hand, ask that your heart might be softened towards him or her and feel the radiant energy of Jesus flowing into your heart and out through it towards the person you have in mind. Picture Jesus filling those areas of hurt with His goodness and allowing His energy to flow into them. May it be your gift – as well as His – to the one you pray for.

*

Exercise Three
Mary Visits Elizabeth

First read the text from chapter 1, verses 39–45 of St Luke's Gospel:

> Mary set out at that time and went as quickly as she could into the hill country to a town in Judah. She went into Zechariah's house and greeted Elizabeth. Now it happened that as soon as Elizabeth heard Mary's greeting, the child leapt in her womb and Elizabeth was filled with the Holy Spirit. She gave a loud cry and said, 'Of all women you are the most blessed, and blessed is the fruit of your womb. Why should I be honoured with a visit from the mother of my Lord? Look, the moment your greeting reached my ears, the child in my womb leapt for joy. Yes, blessed is she who believed that the promise made her by the Lord would be fulfilled'.

Settle yourself now, and listen for any sounds you may be able to hear outside the room you are working in. Just focus on sounds. What can you hear? Notice the sound of the wind or motor cars passing by. You are likely to pick up numerous sounds creeping into your awareness so try to distinguish between those different sounds insofar as you can. Unless you are in a particularly quiet part of the country you are likely to hear the low murmur of conversations outside your room where others may be working or playing. Next draw your attention inwards to the room where you are seated. Try to listen for any sounds that exist within your prayer space. You may notice the hum of background music, or perhaps the noise created by others seated nearby. After a little while, bring your attention still further inwards to listen for any tiny sound made by your own breath moving in and out of your body. If you are particularly still for a moment, you may be able to sense the beat of your own heart as it works away inside you.

When you are ready, begin to sketch in your imagination the Gospel scene described above. Our Blessed Lady has set out on her visit to Elizabeth and you go there to eavesdrop on their conversation. You can concentrate on whatever aspect of their meeting you find helpful but the following suggestions may be helpful. Keep your eye on Elizabeth and watch how she seems very tuned in to the fact that Christ is nearby. What was it about Mary that hinted at the celestial presence within her? What practices did Elizabeth make use of in her own life to ensure that glimpses of the Divine did not pass her by unnoticed? Ask that you might be similarly observant when Christ offers Himself to you.

*

Exercise Four
The Disciples in the Upper Room

First read the text from chapter 2, verses 1–4, of The Acts of the Apostles:

> When Pentecost day came round, they had all met together, when suddenly there came from heaven a sound as of a violent wind which filled the entire house in which they were sitting; and there appeared to them tongues as of fire. These separated and came to rest on the head of each of them. They were all filled with the Holy Spirit and began to speak different languages as the Spirit gave them power to express themselves.

First light a candle in the centre of your prayer space and either seat yourself comfortably or find a spot to lie out horizontally. Now relax and in your own time concentrate on your breathing. Don't force anything. Just allow yourself to drift into an awareness of your breath pattern. Every time you feel yourself drifting off elsewhere or into distractions, take your thoughts gently back to an awareness of what is happening as you breathe. Sometimes it helps to keep up a running commentary on what is going on as you try this exercise. Speak to yourself saying, 'Now I'm breathing in, now I'm breathing out' and you may notice after a while that your pace of breath has slowed down somewhat. This 'slowing down' process is usually noticeable if you are engaged in prayerful meditation over a weekend's workshop. The change of pace is quite discernible and your whole being seems to move into a slower rhythm. After a little practice, you will sharpen the awareness of your breathing pattern. As you engage in this practice, don't change the pace or depth of your breathing. Just observe and key into your breathing rhythm. If you are praying with others in a group setting, keep your eyes closed. You do this for a reason. It is very distracting to find yourself peeking at others to see how they are getting along as you try to pray yourself. It is even more off-putting if you sense that your companions are keeping an eye on your efforts.

After you have been engaged in this activity for a little while, try to see if you can notice any tension building up inside you. Help yourself in this respect by first tightening up the muscles in your face. Hold that posture for a second, and then relax. Next move on to your shoulders and your neck. Tighten up the muscles there for a moment. Hold that stress for a moment and again relax. Now go to the chest and stomach muscles and tighten them. Hold it there for a few moments before relaxing.

As you complete these exercises, imagine that – as you lie on the floor or sit in a chair – you are sinking farther and farther into the ground. When you are ready, move your awareness on to your hands. Make a ball of your fist. Hold that position for a moment before releasing and relaxing. In all of this, make sure that you are as comfortable as possible. If any part of you is under pressure try to relax. Feel the floor underneath you. Imagine it supports you just as God has supported you all the days of your life. Quietly recite the prayer, 'O God, You know me inside and out, through and through. You know every thought that I take and every move that I make. You know them all, Lord, even before they happen. Nothing concerning me is hidden from Your eyes. I ask that You deliver me, Lord, from anything that may hurt or destroy me. Guide me along Your path'.

With each breath inhalation, feel your muscles relaxing and your body becoming heavier. Relax into the arms of Mother Earth and imagine that, while there, you are completely supported, protected, and nurtured by a loving Mother. Try and make sure that any distracting thoughts are given short shrift – just float in that sense of well-being. With eyes almost shut, pick out the candle flame in the dim light. See the candlelight transform itself into golden splinters of light emitting from the candle. The flame transforms itself into tiny sparks. Imagine this is the spirit of God and as you inhale, tell yourself that you are breathing in the life-giving energy of the Lord. As the Spirit gives Himself to you, He gathers up and soothes all the heaviness, pain, stress, gloom and negative emotions that may be part of your experience at the moment. As you exhale, try to imagine all those negative emotions leaving your body. Each in breath brings with it joy and lightness, courage and fortitude. Pray that each out breath takes away with it whatever negative emotions remain.

For a little while, think about the disciples gathered together in the upper room after the crucifixion. Many of them had reached their lowest ebb. The gift they were about to receive was a pearl beyond price. The Holy Spirit was going to replace their hopelessness and despondency by giving them hope and dynamism. I spend the time of my prayer asking for that very same gift for myself.

*

EXERCISE FIVE
An 'Outdoors' Exercise

Find a place outdoors where you can be undisturbed. Sit on the ground and close your eyes. Pay attention as you sit and find out how you are feeling today. Does the sun feel warm on your skin or can you sense the gentle touch of a cool breeze on your cheek? Notice all the details, and attempt to keep your attention on each moment. Now, extend your attention to your other senses and note your surroundings. Put your ears to work, listening for any birdsong you can hear. Also use your power of smell to take in the scent of new mown grass or hay.

After this preparatory phase – during which you have tried to build up a picture of the place in your imagination – begin to fantasise. Imagine that a sort of transparent screen is coming down before your eyes and this screen is becoming more and more opaque as you look at it. Now, as you gaze, you slowly become aware that a form is starting to appear and, as you watch, the form becomes more and more defined. What is beginning to take shape is the symbol of whatever it is you want to work with or change within yourself. As you watch, this thing you want to change becomes more defined and clear. Note the details of your symbol. Perhaps you might notice its colour, or any sounds associated with it. When you are ready, see if this image on the screen is willing to shift or change in any way. See if it wishes to move in any direction. No need to push or pull it. Just let it transform itself if it wants to and if you want to. If it doesn't, that's all right. In fact it may be a good thing to know that this is not a time for change. However, if it does want to adjust and modify, just watch as this change takes place, observing the transformation with all your senses. As you approach the conclusion of the exercise, you may begin to notice that the image on the screen is gently fading. Now bring yourself back to the present moment and relax for a few moments. Focus your attention from head to toe, noticing if there has been any shift in the way you feel. When you are ready, finish the exercise.

The Ox and the Man Gone out of Sight

CHAPTER 7

THE DARKER SIDE

Pain is life, the sharper the pain, the more evidence of life
— Charles Lamb

Recently I began work as a university chaplain and shortly after I began, it was decided that the college should open up a Book of Remembrance to honour deceased alumni of the institution. This book would be placed in a prominent position to celebrate the lives of all those who had died while at college. To this end a religious service was organised and the families of all those concerned were invited. The occasion was terrifically moving. It quickly became apparent that those related to deceased students and staff appreciated deeply the fact that the university was going to honour their friends and relatives in a permanent way. What struck me, however, was that many of the people who attended that evening had extremely painful memories deep within them. They were honouring and remembering their deceased but they were also touching in to the pain that life itself often throws up. This brought home to me forcefully an issue that I am not too keen to dwell on. Life, by its very nature, tends to produce pain. You don't have to go looking for trouble. It has a habit of making its way to your door of its own accord. Some of this pain and grief happens naturally and you only have to think of how death visits all families at one time or another or how natural disasters have a distressing habit of occurring at regular intervals. There is little we can do to prevent such happenings. However quite an amount of our anguish and distress is self-inflicted. At first sight, this seems strange. Who would want to inflict trouble on themselves?

I recall travelling along a road in Canada on one occasion. The route was rather worn and heavily rutted. Clearly large logging trucks used the track regularly and these had gouged out long ruts that ran for several miles. At one point I noticed a sign on the side of the road that simply said, 'Be careful which rut you get into; you may be in it for a very long time'. The sign writer obviously knew how difficult it is to get out of a rut once you find yourself in it. The ruts are danger-points that may be fairly obvious to any outside observer but they can be remarkably hidden to those most intimately concerned. We may be blind to danger signs through a lack of self-awareness or because a realisation is slowly dawning on us. Tiny glimmers of insight may break through our consciousness telling us that change is needed in our lives, but change usually involves suffering as well as sacrifice and these are not elements that people are keen to take on board enthusiastically. Christ himself was not slow to pinpoint this truth, as many of those who came to see him with difficulties and requests were quick to find out. They were confronted with a simple question. 'Do you want to change?' or 'Do you want to be well?' This question was often backed away from. I cannot say I blame the visitors.

Try to do a little better. In your prayer time, take a positive step backward to get things into better perspective. Ask yourself if there are areas in your life where you feel stuck or stymied. If your answer is in the affirmative, take a further step. The next issue that needs to be faced is – are you prepared to do something constructive to unblock the bottleneck within? Unblocking usually means that a price has to be paid before forward progress can be achieved and the number and variety of ways we can find blockages along our path are legion. The list includes; memories of past failures, fear, shame, anger, or sheer bloody-mindedness. These are just starters, but any one of them might provide a useful heading to begin self-reflection. Simply observe, to begin with, how you are feeling and note how your body is performing. That simple exercise, in itself, can be an effective way of generating the reflective process.

One honest individual whom I know quite well told me that he suffered fairly regularly from back trouble. When asked to look at why the pain might be occurring, he at once perceived that it seemed to flare up at exceptionally troublesome moments in his stressful job. The worry and anxiety he encountered in his job seemed to be transforming themselves into physical discomfort and ailments. Once he acknowledged that, his road to recovery began.

I observed something fairly similar within myself not so long ago. I was asked to take up residence in a tough, inner-city area and at the time of the request, I was doing two jobs simultaneously. That meant that I really had my hands full. Shortly after I took up residence in this perilous environment I began to notice a fairly constant queasy feeling in my stomach. This queasiness went on for some months but I tried to damp down the feeling. I put off asking myself what it might mean for as long as I could. When, finally, the feeling of unease reached almost unbearable levels, I was lucky enough to get a quiet week away in the country. Only then did I begin to pray about what had been going on. Three or four days of quiet prayerful pondering produced little, but finally, something cracked – and I don't think it was me. Three little sentences began to bring themselves to the surface of my consciousness. The first sentence that began to play itself like a recurring theme in my mind was, 'You're sick'. A day or two later, this phrase was followed by a second. 'Something needs to change'. Towards the end of the week a final idea forcibly presented itself. 'You're the something that needs to change'. The sentences, when combined, were like a sort of megaphone message and seemed to me almost like the following image or picture which kept playing over in my mind.

Quite close to where I live there is a motorway that makes its way out towards the Irish coastline. You can make your way off the motorway into little villages at various points along the route but, if you try to get back from these small towns to the highway, you are faced with a choice of two routes. One allows you to re-entry the motorway easily, but the other, if you try to take it, suddenly brings you face to face with a gigantic road sign. This billboard is massive and intimidating and contains a simple two-word warning: 'Go Back'. The sign is trying to explain that if you continue on the way you are going – a catastrophe awaits. You will indeed get back to the motorway – but you will find yourself heading against the flow of traffic. That's the scenario that kept presenting itself to me in image form during my week of reflection. The queasy feeling in my stomach was a sort of warning sign. It was trying to roar out a caution – 'Go Back'. Change the way you are living or the way you are living will change you. Although it's painful and an unwelcome task, it's not a bad idea to ask yourself occasionally if there are 'Go Back' signs in your own life. If there are, what might these 'Go Back' signs be? The first obvious barometer is your body. Like a car engine, it may seize up if you are working it too hard or refusing to give it sufficient rest and relaxation. Although it may not be immediately obvious, your body is usually a friendly agent even if at times this requires it to become ill for your own good as this may be the only way it has of slowing down. Do a spot-check for a moment and ask yourself if your body is trying to tell you anything.

Now move on to the spiritual plane. How has my spirit been recently? Have good or bad habits been co-existing within me and if so, what has their legacy been? Look at these traits and note where and how they operated before judging whether they produced consolation or desolation within you. Take your time with this examination because you cannot fix what you do not first face. You may be struck by the similarity of the question facing you and the query Christ placed before his followers. What does a person do when good and bad habits of theirs seem closely intertwined – when the weeds and the wheat grow together? Christ suggested that, on occasions, we might have to accept the shadow side of our personality, along with the more positive aspects, if growth is to occur. Allowing that sort of co-existence within is all very well, but it's hazardous as it may mask or cloud the need for radical action and promote laziness or procrastination. It may also stifle our own inner voice or allow the voices of others to have undue influence.

Anthony de Mello regularly cautioned against allowing others hold excessive sway over us. It meant, he said, listening to their voices and their standards instead of our own. A person who trims himself to fit everybody else's standards will soon whittle himself or herself down to nothing. Set out your own stall. Be aware of what truly brings you life for if you are unsure of this you can become – in Anthony de Mello's phrase – like a little monkey responding to any and all voices that surround you. Right from our earliest beginnings we hear the claps of praise, or the 'boos' of derision, from those around us and this creates a sort of dependency which is almost like a drug. This pill might be labelled 'the need for approval' and if it takes over our lives we are more or less finished, even before we have begun. We begin to seek attention, success, appreciation, prestige, power, and we do this with a sense of desperation. If the need for approval takes a really strong grip it isn't long before we dread losing the respect of others. Try to notice if this trend exists within you. It's not uncommon.

Shortly after the Second World War, many people wondered how a large proportion of the German nation could allow itself be influenced in their modes of behaviour by a small group of perverted leaders. How could a whole group of people allow itself be blinded about its best and worst instincts? In order to try and come up with some answers, an experiment was conducted whereby a number of individuals were asked to gather in a room and conduct an uncomplicated experiment. A number of lines of various lengths were drawn on a wall and the assembled volunteers were asked to grade them according to length. They were to start by saying which was the longest line and work their way down to the shortest. The whole experiment was filmed so that objective observers could view the result. What the volunteers did not know was that imposters had been placed in their midst who knew the true purpose of the experiment. A number of these imposters were initially asked to indicate which they felt was the longest line. The first imposter indicated which line he felt was the longest. His choice was obviously much shorter than some of the alternatives and the true volunteers can be seen on film sniggering among themselves at his obvious mistake. However, the second volunteer – also a stooge planted by those conducting the experiment – indicated the same choice as his co-conspirator. Now the true volunteers can be seen on film looking at each other questioningly. Maybe their eyesight is deceiving them? Perhaps what they first considered to be the longest line is incorrect. If they give their true opinion they may leave themselves open to ridicule. You can almost smell the tension rising as you watch the film. The potential risk of losing their dignity is there for all to see. When the third contestant – who was also a 'plant' – was asked for his opinion and indicated the same choice as his first two companions, the true volunteers are clearly stunned. Finally, one of the rightful volunteers is asked to indicate which line he thinks is longest. Dubiously, and with hesitation, he pauses before giving his reply. Then at last he points his finger. With obvious reluctance, he votes for the same line as the others have chosen. He has been cowed. He's not prepared to stand behind what he truly believes. The other genuine volunteers, when asked in their turn, go down the same road. They sheepishly make the same choice even though clearly, when they started the experiment, they had little doubt what the correct answer was. Peer-group pressure, or an unwillingness to look foolish, had swayed them in their decision-making. They wanted and needed the approval of their peers and this convinced them to act against their better judgement. They let the opinion of others prejudice what they honestly believed themselves. It's not unusual for us to do the same. We take on board stray comments and opinions from all quarters and give them much more prominence than we ought. We even allow them to disturb our peace.

How often have you been brought high or low by an ill-considered or evil-intentioned remark from those around you? You may have heard others mention that you are putting on weight, or ageing rapidly, or going a little grey, or not looking as perky as usual. How much have the comments affected you? Quite a lot, probably. If you weren't feeling a little down in the dumps before you heard the remarks, you certainly will be afterwards. Such a little thing – if we are over-reliant on the opinions of others – can puff us up or down mightily. St Augustine recommended that we do not let our happiness depend on such shallow or transient things for such euphoria can hardly be called happiness at all. Ultimately, it is the Lord we are trying to please and in Him lies our contentment. We may, if we are not careful, lose our equilibrium through over-reliance on the opinion of others but might it be possible – with a little innovative thinking – to use apprehension and fear in a constructive way? Can we make use of something that seems so destructive to bring us closer to God?

Dr Sheila Cassidy, well known for both her prose and her courageous work among the poor of Chile, suggests that this might be a possibility. In her writings, she recalls how one day she treated a wounded peasant who stumbled across her path. He had been shot by the secret police but was so terrified of their reputation that he refused to go to hospital. She therefore treated him privately, but her generous action as a doctor was noted in the local community and she was betrayed to the authorities. This led to her arrest and subsequent torture. In jail, she did not divulge any information about the sick peasant whom she had treated, even though she thought she was going to die. She did manage to draw something worthwhile from her suffering, because she allied it to the sufferings of Christ. In some small way she believed she was experiencing what Christ Himself had experienced and in this way felt enormously loved by God because – however minutely – she was sharing in His son's suffering.

In much the same way, others endure and undergo pain and give the experience significance by offering it up as atonement. Most of us are not as fearlessly unselfish. Our usual first reaction is to run from adversity. With effort, though, it may be possible to view life's anguished moments, not as an occasion for flight, but rather as an opportunity to purify our hearts. St Ignatius of Loyola suggests that the path to holiness can be illuminated by struggle. For this to happen we must look at our own pain, failures, disappointments and sins but before we start out it is advisable to remember that the Father, Son and Holy Spirit love us more than we can possibly imagine despite any faults and failings which we note in ourselves. After we acknowledge that sin and weakness are part of our inheritance, we should begin to look towards Christ for reassurance and hope. We can do this by walking with Christ through His passion and thinking about the Second Person of the Trinity who suffered and was crucified for us. Having thought about the failure, we now turn our attention towards the future. We think about the Easter of our lives. We, as Dr Cassidy was keen on mentioning, should be an Easter people who can deal with failure constructively. Many, however, find this almost impossible and are overwhelmed by it. The powers of darkness have such a grip that coming into the light hardly seems possible. The suffering they have to endure leaves them feeling lost and forgotten, disconnected and alone. As well as this, the anguish of feeling misused and manipulated often leads to feelings of resentment and self-pity. Our emotional balance can be brittle and fragile. Those who read the New Testament often mention that they are surprised how often the texts speak about a dark power in the universe and the fact that life and death, darkness and light, co-exist so proportionately. Without God's grace, that balance can be blown out of equilibrium in our minds and we begin to believe that things will never get better or that they will never be right again. It's easy to believe that the world is conspiring against us or to fear that we are being dragged down by life's misfortunes and becoming dysfunctional. In that scenario, we become like damaged people and act like them also, blaming everybody but ourselves for what is going wrong in our lives. De Mello used to say that in such a dysfunctional state, we are, in a sense, asleep. Even more frighteningly, we don't want to wake up. We don't want to be happy. At first sight, this statement seems ridiculous and de Mello, when he made it, certainly shocked his audience. With a twinkle in his eye he would encourage them to undertake a little test. Think of somebody you love very much. Then, in your imagination, say to that person that – if you had to make a choice – you would rather have happiness than your mutual close friendship. That exercise seems easy enough to undertake, but most of the audiences at de Mello's workshops couldn't achieve it. They felt selfish and were unable to let such a sentiment rise to the surface. De Mello would laugh and say, 'See how we've been brainwashed. No true friend would demand that you choose him or her above your own happiness'.

*

Exercise One
The Unprepared Beginning

Find a place you like for prayer where you will not be disturbed. Now close your eyes and begin to fix your awareness on what you are doing. Feel a chair underneath you as you sit and become aware of how it supports your weight. Next move your attention to the air that you breathe. Notice the cool feel of that air on the tip of your nostrils. If you are praying outside, or near a sunny window, become aware of the sun's warmth as it caresses your skin. If the sun is absent, be aware instead of any cool breeze that may caress you as you work.

Sometimes we can make the very experiences we have in life into a meditation. To do this, you start by going back over the past few months and seeing if any incident stands out.

One such occasion came up for me recently when I met with a friend. She was keen to undertake a pilgrimage experience and so was I.

Almost immediately an enthusiasm for the idea caught us both simultaneously. She wanted to plan the whole walk out very methodically whereas I was much keener to just jump in and get started. We could see what detailed plans might be needed for the venture as we went along. I suppose I was a bit scared that if we went through each little aspect of the walk and tried to anticipate every conceivable problem, the enormity of the undertaking might eventually put us off.

For this type of prayerful and reflective exercise, you just go back over an incident in your mind, asking what it might have to teach you. Are you usually impulsive about what you do? Does that trait help or hinder you?

By letting you mind roam over incidents from your past, you should be able to think of other situations where you had to follow through on an idea. Did you jump into the situation in the way described above, or hold back?

If you did hold back, what were your reasons for doing so? Was it to consider all the angles of the project carefully before weighing up your options?

By holding back and reflecting for a longer period, did you finally – insofar as you can judge from past results – come to a wise decision?

Or did you spend so long prevaricating that you came to no conclusion at all and let the possibility of action slip through your fingers?

Only you, in all honesty, can answer those questions truthfully for yourself and the honesty with which you answer them will guide you in future decision-making.

*

EXERCISE TWO
Renewed Life

First read the text from chapter 24, verses 36–43 of St Luke's Gospel:

> They were still talking about all this when Jesus Himself stood among them
> and said to them, 'Peace be with you'. In a state of alarm and fright, they
> thought they were seeing a ghost. But He said, 'Why are you so agitated, and
> why are these doubts stirring in your hearts? See by my hands and my feet
> that it is I myself. Touch me and see for yourselves. A ghost has no flesh and
> bones as you can see I have'. And as He said this He showed them His hands
> and His feet. Their joy was so great that they still could not believe it, as
> they were dumbfounded. He then said to them, 'Have you anything here to
> eat?' And they offered Him a piece of grilled fish, which He took and ate
> before their eyes.

Sit comfortably and alone in a quiet room. As soon as you are ready, listen for any sounds you can hear outside the room and as you do so, try
to distinguish any different elements you can make out within the overall noise. It's possible you can hear the wind, or a bird, or traffic or some
other noise outside. After a few moments, draw the focus of your attention into the room. Listen for whatever sounds you can hear within. You
may hear the ticking of a clock, or the sound of others who are engaged
in the meditation. Just note those sounds. After a little while, bring the
focus of your attention still further inwards. Become aware of the coolness of the air as it comes into your nostrils and listen for the gentle
sound that it makes as it enters.

When you feel stilled and settled, allow the Gospel story I have
described above settle in your mind. Imagine Jesus is there with you and
ask Him to place you at the scene. He might relate how His followers
were that morning, for a sense of doom and gloom had settled upon them
after His own brutal death. Probably the disciples feared something similar might happen to each one of them. They hardly had the strength to
wake up and face a new day. Ask Jesus why He let them get so low in
themselves. Was it because, as Charles Lamb said, 'pain is life, the sharper the pain, the more evidence of life', or to let them know, as Ernest
Hemingway was fond of saying, that 'the world breaks everyone, and
afterwards many are strong at the broken places'?

Ask that you may glimpse those same disciples when they first sense
that Christ is back amongst them. Watch particularly for the ray of hope
in their faces and the slow dawning of a realisation that perhaps everything is not lost after all. Remember the times when you felt very low

yourself and ask if there is anything in your life or behaviour that needs to change if new hope and growth is to happen for you. Ask God to show you how you can put your best foot forward into the future. Decide when you will implement that first step.

When you are ready to finish, pause for a moment and again become aware of your breathing. Listen for the breath as it comes into your body. Now allow your awareness to float outwards and listen for sounds in the room. After this, focus your attention still farther outwards and listen for sounds outside the room. This will draw your awareness back to the present moment and away from your inner self, after which you can quietly bring your meditation to a close.

*

Exercise Three
Come and See

First read the story from chapter 2 of St John's Gospel:

> One day, two of the disciples were in John the Baptist's company when suddenly Jesus passed quite close by their group. When the two friends asked who this new arrival was, John told them that they should approach Him themselves and ask. They began to follow Jesus at a distance but He turned and spotted them and so they had to ask, 'Rabbi, where are you staying?' He told them to come and see and so they went and saw where He stayed and spent the rest of that day with Him.

Now begin. It may take you a little time to get into a prayerful atmosphere and things may not be as perfect as you had hoped, but at least you have taken the first step. As you inhale, try to relax and be at peace with yourself. Become aware of any noises you can hear outside the room you are praying in. Just focus on those noises and see if you can use them to build an aura of peace around yourself. Then bring your attention inwards to focus on the various sounds that might be present within the room. Pick out the various shades of noise you notice. Next, bring your attention deep within yourself. Try to see if you can spot the very tiny sound of your own breath as it enters your body. You may begin to become aware of the slight coolness of the air on the tip of your nose as it is drawn deep down into your being.

Now build up the story in your mind, as if it were a movie being played inside your head. You are with one of your closest companions. For months now you have been in the company of John the Baptist because he seemed to bring a sense of purpose to your life. Now the day of reckoning has come. Christ has appeared, but whether that will make a difference to your life or not is unclear. Something is been offered, but does not have to be accepted. Firstly, notice the appearance of Jesus. He comes into the picture slowly. Only John seems to notice the significance at first. Something – or someone – prompts you to ask about the stranger. What prompted you? Now you are told to go over and check Him over for yourself. Not an easy task and, you might say, rather embarrassing. But you do pick up the courage to approach Christ and – even better – when He offers His invitation you may be like the disciples in the story. You may go with Him for the day to see what He has to offer. It's as if we can go into our deepest centre, the core of our being. A place we seldom go.

As you start, you realise you have to leave the tried and tested. You need to let go of John the Baptist. This will not be easy because he has been a good guide and teacher who has taught you much. He has been something solid to lean on. Such supports are not easy to cut yourself free from. Your journey will take on new challenges and new directions. The beginnings may not be easy, and the end is as yet completely un-known. When will your journey end? Will you find what you are looking for? Do you even know what you are seeking? You are on a journey or a search. That much you probably know. It's part of the reason why you might be prepared to leave John the Baptist and take risks. You seek someone with vision and a purpose in life.

The search is why I left John the Baptist and why I took risks. I am looking for someone with vision, with a purpose in life. What was the hardest challenge you faced when you were with John the Baptist? What was the best part of the last few months, as you tried to share the mission?

Now finish the meditation and relax.

CHAPTER 8

THERE IS LIFE AFTER DEATH

It is always in the midst, in the epicentre of your troubles that
you find serenity
— Antoine de Saint-Exupéry

A few years ago, I planned a summer trip to Calcutta, India, to work with some street children. I was part of a team that ran a youth retreat centre at the time and in order to bring some funds to the Indian project some members of the Retreat House came up with a bright 'fundraising' idea. They suggested, first, that we should hold an 'India style' meal and ask for donations from those who attended. They followed this up by recommending that we should include in the evening a feature that I had not come across before. In essence the idea was simple, though it was imperative that those who agreed to come neither knew of the notion nor were told anything about it in advance.

At the start of the evening three very large tables were to be put in place before people arrived at the venue. Each table had a sign or symbol placed on it. One was called the 'star' table, another the 'triangle' table and the third had a 'square' placed on it. As each guest arrived, they were given a ticket with a square, a triangle or a star. The idea was that you were meant to find, and then sit at, your respective table as soon as you arrived. This people did, and soon the meal began.

Those who had organised and were serving the meal first came in with platters of delicious food and headed for the 'star' table. They served that table with every delicacy imaginable and then quickly came in with a second selection of dishes that was a little less delicious. This they presented to the 'square' table guests. Finally the waiters came in with a third set of serving dishes. These held very basic fare indeed and were served to those who sat at the 'triangle' table. Very little comment was passed at first for I think people believed that the fancier food had probably run out, and they were a little embarrassed for the organisers. What they didn't know was that the meal – or perhaps more precisely, the evening – contained a hidden message within it. In the mind of the organisers, visitors were grouped into sectors. They were either part of the First World, the Second World, or the Third World and whichever group each individual guest belonged to had been decided rather arbitrarily – in this case by which type of ticket you had picked up at the door. Those tickets marked you down for the 'star', 'square' or 'triangle' sector or table. Depending on which table you sat at you were going to be treated like a king, an ordinary citizen, or a beggar.

Murmurs of unrest first raised their ugly heads about halfway through the meal or at least that's when those serving noticed the atmosphere becoming decidedly chilly. I suspect the message of 'class' and 'class treatment' only began to sink home in dribs and drabs. Dessert was served. Once again, those at the 'star' table got their helpings before anyone else as waiters appeared from all sides bearing dishes of baked Alaska. The 'square' table was served next and they found themselves receiving ice cream and jelly. Not as nice as the first table, perhaps, but still not bad. After an interval, the servers returned. This time they had some bananas with them. These they threw casually onto the 'triangle' table as they passed by.

The message was now stark and brutal and those at the third table began to object. They had contributed as much financially as everybody else and saw no reason why they should be treated so despicably. Some of the guests at the 'star' table – not many, but a few – noticed the plight of their bottom table 'cousins' and wandered over with their surplus goodies. However, this didn't appease those in the marginalised positions and the more rowdy elements among them began to make their way to the top table to grab what they could. The rest of the evening is shrouded in a sort of dark mist for me. All I can say for certain is that the atmosphere turned decidedly nasty and mulish and mutterings about 'getting even' started to rise to the surface.

Afterwards, as part of the evening's entertainment, a film about street children and the way they lived and survived in Calcutta was shown. The plan was that a discussion would be conducted to finish off the proceedings, during which the whole group would reflect on what had happened during the meal. This never happened. Those at the third table believed – with some justification – that they had been treated abominably. One or two of them were so incensed that, during the film, they took to kicking the electric plug of the video machine out of the wall. They were determined that their feelings would not go unnoticed and not to put too fine a point on it, we had to abandon the remaining part of the evening. To tell the truth, the organisers felt that they were lucky to escape without a minor riot developing.

As I reflected upon this event afterwards, it seemed to me that an atmosphere something akin to evil had taken over the proceedings. The meal, and those who attended it, had brought an ugly home truth to the surface. A section of the crowd had been dealt an unfair hand, but that's not unusual. Most of us, at some stage in our lives, will suffer something similar and feel hard done by. Such situations, if pondered upon, may have lessons to teach us. How we react to those lessons tells us a lot about ourselves and, if we examine our reactions to any such adverse episodes in our lives, we will receive enlightenment. Those who allow resentment about such injustices to fester within them will find that the result will be unmitigated disaster. What's important is not so much the action we have been through, but rather our reaction. If we don't or can't forgive and let go our resentment, the persons most damaged by our subsequent behaviour will be ourselves.

It's not easy to reflect on unhappy or painful experiences in our lives, and drawing something constructive from such experiences is easier said than done. Remarkable balance is needed, as well as a degree of awareness of our own limitations. One who had such balance – Sophocles, the ancient Greek philosopher – was said to be the wisest man alive in his time, but he said of himself that he only had the reputation for wisdom because he realised how ignorant he really was. That's the level of self-awareness we are after but not many human beings attain such heights of wisdom or astuteness. Most lock themselves into mind-sets and see little hope of gaining insight from the darker episodes that befall them in life. Most of us suspect that if something bad happens, then very little of value is likely to emerge. Thus we find it inconceivable that unfortunate incidents that befall us might contain hidden fruit – if reflected upon. We forget that irksome grains of sand are constantly needed within oysters if a pearl is to be produced and the fact that we try to eradicate as many early painful memories from our lives as possible means that gaining 'pearls of wisdom' from our more difficult daily experiences is an extremely unusual occurrence. Our programming manages to persuade us that our 'shadow side' is unlikely to be productive and we sense that our early failures are likely to be repeated.

Listening to an inner voice of hope is not easy. That voice might whisper words of encouragement and even indicate ways of moving forward positively in our lives but it is not a voice that comes for free. It takes a lot of hard work and courage to know who you are and what you want. Looking for the silver lining in dark situations often requires subtlety and an ability not to beat yourself up. Human beings are like flowers. They open and are receptive to softly falling dew but protect themselves and close immediately when violent rain threatens. That's the way the average human reacts as well and so we have to be constantly on the alert for likely 'growth areas' as and when they occur. Unfortunately, it's easier, as a general rule, to be aware of where failure might crop up than to turn our attention to likely opportunities for success. Instead of putting the emphasis on our strengths, we turn our attention more readily to our weaknesses.

This was demonstrated to me very neatly recently when one of Ireland's most famous former soccer players – Johnny Giles – was interviewed on local radio. He was asked how he managed to get the best out of himself. I found his reply both honest and illuminating. He modestly explained that many players that were potentially better than himself never, as far as he could see, seemed to achieve true greatness. Worse than that, they didn't get anything like they deserved out of their talents. He continued: 'I tell you what I found about really great players when I was on the pitch myself. The really good ones knew what they could do with a football and had the confidence to exploit their talent. More importantly, they knew what they couldn't do and didn't try the impossible. Bad players, on the other hand, seemed to always try to do what they knew in reality they couldn't. They compounded this error by not doing the simple things they were well capable of. In the end they achieved little or nothing – they made a dog's dinner of their talent'. Giles said that in his opinion, this trait didn't just apply to football players. It seemed to him that it also spread to many different professions. People insist on attempting to do things they just can't while ignoring or not doing what they are perfectly capable of. Consequently, they achieve much less than they should.

Allowing the shadow side of our personalities to gain the upper hand in our lives is something we all have to guard and fight against. The famed spiritual writer, Henri Nouwen, said this point was driven home to him time and time again while reflecting on his own life. He said prayer helped him recognise his own weaknesses as well as his strengths. There was hardly a day in his life when some dark cloud didn't drift by. By means of prayer and reflection, he recognised the darkness or depression for what it was and refused to stick his head in such gloomy surroundings. The trick, he found, was to spot the darkness as it came towards him and, by cleverly anticipating where such patches of gloom might crop up, get himself out of the way quickly and thus avoid such potentially harmful places. In this way, he didn't allow impending sadness to grow into the characteristic he feared most – depression.

A friend of mine, who happens to be a noted spiritual director, recently mentioned a number of reasons why some of his students were reluctant to make use of such wisdom. He has to work with novices in a religious order and mentioned that they often find it difficult to see silver linings at the edges of their dark clouds and he wondered why. He knew that C. S. Lewis was fond of pointing out that good and evil coexist side by side in our world and the two seem to be forever jostling for position. It's as if God and the devil are constantly in conflict. God stimulates the good that we do but Satan and his cohorts have a different plan in mind. Their job is to annoy, frustrate and distract at every turn, and if they can instil fear and hopelessness into those who attempt to turn their face towards God's kingdom, so much the better.

St Ignatius turns his spotlight on the struggle between the protagonists for good and evil in his book of spiritual exercises. He noted that, in life, disappointments and dark clouds are encountered by everyone. Satan knows this only too well and uses this fact to set up his game plan. If he can disillusion us and stop us in our tracks, he knows that progress in prayer will be slow or nonexistent.

My novice-master friend also suggested to his charges a second reason exists that might account for lack of progress in prayer. The rays of hope and moments of consolation that exist in some people's lives are so well hidden or unrecognised by the individuals themselves that they are almost invisible. He said a third possible cause for not seeing potential in life's difficulties is that we might be blinded by our own anger. No one likes to acknowledge that anger exists within him or her. For most of us, however, that feature is a painful reality. So how might we wisely handle our anger?

As he spoke to the novices, my friend hinted that three possible steps might be constructively used. First of all, we have to 'own' our own anger. Secondly, we need to understand where it comes from and why. Only then, when these two stages have been reached, can we begin to deal with our inner fury. Most human beings seem to contain pockets of suppressed rage. I know I have difficulty owning up to this trait within myself for it seems a very unattractive characteristic. It expresses itself at times in suppression, assertiveness, aggression, or even violence. We hate these elements within ourselves and try to deny them. Somewhere in the deep recesses of our memories we understand dimly that the past we have gone through, while it undoubtedly had its areas of enrichment, left us with dark shadow areas that haunt our present.

Some of our earliest memories may not have been good. They may have been frightening or gloomy and may have left behind them a deposit of inner sadness. Such sadness is an affliction of the heart and – if it is allowed develop into depression – may well become an affliction of the soul. Have you, at any time, encountered impossible stress, loss or need and if so, has it deposited an unhealthy residue within you? Think about times of stress in your life and chew over the frustrations that caused it.

Next move on to loss. What have been the losses in your life? For most of us there are a number of inevitable losses and these may include youth, independence, authority, health, or possibly the loss of a loved one. If I try to select one of these losses, perhaps the most natural one to settle on, though definitely painful, is death and bereavement. A normal bereavement, according to the experts, might last about three months, so has my sense of loss gone on for longer than that? These experts say that if the feeling of depression goes on for more than six months it's time to look at yourself. It may be that we are not seeing beyond the death and darkness. We have forgotten that, for Christians, the darkness normally associated with death is supposed to lead, in due course, towards the light.

This point occurred to me recently when I was asked to undertake a difficult task. A mother gave birth to a premature baby, which was found to be dead when it was taken from the womb, and the funeral directors asked me to conduct a very quiet burial service as that was the mother's wish. The undertaker picked me up in the hearse at the entrance to the graveyard and, being a easy-going individual, he chatted pleasantly as we made our way towards the open grave. His conversation was aimed towards trying to make me feel at home in his environment and quite casually he said, 'You know my clients never complain about the sort of service the clergyman provides. It's good to know that there is nothing that can be done to you, or with you, or about you after you are dead that will do you much good or much harm'. His sentiments stopped me short. What he said made sense from one viewpoint right enough – but not from a Christian's point of view. In fact it is the very opposite to what the Christian is supposed to believe about living and dying.

For a Christian, death is not final; it is not the end. In reality, it is a new beginning. It allows us to retain optimism because we believe something greater follows. A new passage of life begins which has wonderful potential for the departed one and for those left behind. Both have tasks to complete. The one who has died continues his or her journey and those left behind can do something to help the departed on their way. Hopefully, when the deceased arrives into the fullness of their glory, they will keep the rest of us in mind and use their newfound position to assist us on our journey. If we bear the darkness with hope and courage, then the darkness may well bear us towards the light and help us remember that a day will come when a group of our friends will go with us to a cemetery and hold a brief and sorrowful service before returning home. All will return home except one, and that one will be you or me, because the event will have been our own funeral.

One group of people who try to draw 'light from the darkness' are recovering alcoholics. Their courage and tenacity are a source of inspiration whenever I work with them and recently I noticed – during a conference I gave – that certain subjects seem to crop up on their agendas whenever they get together. The themes of pain, loss, sadness, self-loathing and anger were all very much to the forefront as people began to tell their individual stories. Almost everyone who stood up to give witness mentioned that they had tried to bury their personal pain in innumerable ways. Some tried drugs, others overwork, while still others used television as a numbing device to dull their pain. A small number even experimented with excessive physical activity as a means of wearing themselves out. If none of these practices worked, those who spoke said they were quite prepared to use alcohol to dull the pain of living. It didn't help. Somewhere, deep down in their being, some small voice kept telling them that all attempts to anaesthetise themselves meant that they would also block out feelings of joy.

It's hard to have a sense of light without some form of shadow for contrast. Anthony de Mello claimed that it is only when sick people realise and accept that they are ill that they have a possibility of recovery and moving on. Only when they become tired of their sickness do they create for themselves an opportunity to move towards health. Many, he said, don't go to their doctor for a cure. They have no interest in being truly fixed up. They are looking primarily for relief from their distress. I know this sounds daft when you first hear it and your first reaction may be disbelief. That certainly was the response of many who attended de Mello workshops and televised retreats. It's very interesting to watch their reactions when they are challenged about the statement on screen. Some are incredulous. Many are angry and refuse to believe that what he is saying could be true. But think it over for yourself. When you have been in trouble and have gone looking for a cure, are you really prepared to take the medicine necessary for a change to occur?

Well, perhaps it might be wiser not to look at your own story. Oftentimes it is easier to look at the situations your friends find themselves in. Judge the truth of the statement by watching them and their actions. It's easier to comprehend and accept difficult truths through the stories of others than your own story. The wisdom of the message is so painful that often we cannot see it mirrored in our own situation. Human beings are suggestible creatures. Oftentimes we don't speak the truth to ourselves. Deep down we fear that if we admit to ourselves that we might be sick, it may limit our ability to start out on the road to recovery. Our mindset may become one of defeat. Hopelessness may turn into a self-fulfilling prophecy as numerous sport-stars and entertainers – who have experienced great success in their chosen profession – are honest enough to admit. Bob Dylan, the tremendously successful American folk singer said that at the very height of his fame he was booed off stage in Fairfax after introducing a new type of music to his audience and it certainly was not pleasant. He was philosophical enough to remark: 'You can't worry about things like that. You're nobody if you don't get booed sometime.'

So, the 'boos' of life are likely to come our way every once in a while. Their importance is not so much that they land on our doorsteps but rather what our reaction to such adversity will be. Saul Alinksy, the American activist, used to say, 'The action is in the reaction' and he was right. How we respond is critical. Do the put-downs stop us in our tracks or encourage us to move forward with greater resolve? Look to Jesus in times of adversity. When individuals with major problems came to the Saviour He seemed to suggest that His job was to empower and encourage movement rather than allow people develop 'stuck state' sort of mentality. He challenged each individual, even though He knew that moving forward is often not fun.

How long has it been since I accepted a challenge in my life and took some risk? Has it been ages since I moved to the margins rather than travelling along the safe centre ground? A wise person does not constantly fear the edges and fringes. He or she studies them, and sometimes explores them, because often it is being out on the periphery that ultimately leads to growth. The edges or margins, it has to be admitted, are often more dangerous than solid centre ground and being out on the extremity, instead of enclosed in the safe centre space, takes a particular kind of courage.

In China, parents often tell children a folk tale to build up or revitalise the type of bravery I am talking about here. They mention that there was once in their land a huge dragon that was greatly feared. It went from village to village, killing cattle and dogs, and didn't stop there. Anything that came into its path was devoured indiscriminately – and that included children. The villagers were so distraught they called upon a wise and good wizard to help them in their predicament. During their discussions, the kindly wizard told them a simple truth: 'I have to be honest and tell you that I cannot slay the dragon, for, magician though I am, I am too afraid myself, but I shall find you a person that will be able to achieve your desire'. With that, he simply transformed himself into a dragon and took up a position on a bridge that led into their town. This meant that all who came to the spot, including the locals who did not know it was the wizard, were petrified, and not one of them was brave enough to pass. Months passed. One day a new traveller happened to pass that way and came up to the bridge. He noticed the dragon but calmly climbed over it before continuing on his journey. As soon as the wizard saw this, he promptly regained his human shape and called after the man, 'Come back, friend, you are the very man I have been waiting for. Your courage is the sort needed to solve our dilemma'. Chinese parents mention that the moral of the story is that the enlightened know that fear is in the way you look at things, not in the things themselves.

So, to travel forward along the edges, and not by the safer central route, a degree of trust is needed, the sort of trust Jesus Himself showed towards His disciples – though not all of them. Jesus knew whom to trust and whom to be doubtful of. He trusted Peter, but not Judas. So ask yourself, 'How is my trust? When have I trusted my gut instincts and been glad I did? Have I been awake to the possibilities around me or asleep?' It takes diligence and practice to stay awake. Be like the locksmith I once kept an eye on as he sat as his table and worked. All the time his senses were alert and alive. A lock had been brought to him but the keys were missing so he just patiently began to juggle around with the lock by poking a piece of wire around inside it. With great attention to detail he listened to every sound the wire made as it was worked inside the lock. The sounds and action meant nothing to me. I saw nothing, heard nothing, or felt nothing but that was because my senses were asleep. The locksmith, on the other hand, was alert and his senses were acutely tuned to the business at hand. Within a short time and under his skilled direction, the lock sprang open. The locksmith had been able to interpret the data before him. His skills had provided the key. Try to let your awareness reap similar benefits for you.

Exercise One
Your Daily Blessings

Settle yourself into a balanced comfortable position and take a few slow, deep breaths. Begin to count silently up to four as you take each breath in and out. Continue with these deep and slow breaths for a couple of minutes. Just be quiet and feel the calmness seep over you as you sense the natural rhythm of your breathing. Sometimes it helps to give yourself a running commentary as you try this exercise. You might go at the same pace as your breathing and tell yourself 'Now I'm breathing in, now I'm breathing out'.

You need to know yourself and what helps you in your prayer. For example, I am influenced by the amount of light around me and know that soft lighting helps my meditation. I think others are similarly affected and find it hard to relax in harsh or bright light. If it's too bright, you might try closing the curtains and putting on a small side lamp. I would not usually try to conduct a meditation with a harsh neon light as my backdrop. Many people use a candle and make use of the soft flickering flame to produce a relaxed state for themselves. You can even focus on the flickering of the flame by half closing your eyes before you begin. In this way you are likely to see tiny slivers of light emanating from the candle and it might assist you if you think of these as the light of the Spirit entering into your inner being.

You might start by saying one of your favourite prayers such as, 'Thank You, Lord, for Your great love' or 'Jesus, remember me, as You come into Your Kingdom'. Remember that God is standing at the door of everybody's heart and as He does so He knocks. Some never hear that knock. Some only hear it as they get older or when they are in serious trouble. Some hear, but don't respond because they fear the price Jesus will ask of them. If they let God in they are afraid they will not enjoy their life. What they fail to recognise is that God is the happiness they are pursuing. If they are attempting to pray, they try to pray upwards, not inwards. For these few moments of prayer, try to imagine Christ actively at work within you and offering His blessings for your benefit. Give thanks for those blessings and ask that you be given the grace you need to respond to His call.

*

Exercise Two
Making Friends with Yourself

Begin by relaxing as usual. As you sit there, begin to think about the body you have been given and the life you manage to live through it. How does it feel when you do that? Try to sense whether you feel joy or sadness as you make your way through this exercise.

Work on developing a response of friendliness and kindness towards yourself. It might help if you use the following prayer: 'How lucky I am, how grateful I am'. It's one Juliana of Norwich used to use. Try to stay with that feeling of being grateful as well as lucky and if the emotion begins to diminish or evaporate patiently work on bringing it back.

Now bring to the forefront of your consciousness the image of a good friend that you have known. Sketch an image of that friend in your mind and do this by recalling how he or she acted towards you in real life – say in a conversation, or an encounter, or an event. It's best if you choose someone who is around your own age and not someone who is much older or younger than yourself. Try to develop feelings of gratefulness and thanks.

Next move on to someone who evokes more neutral feelings than the friend imagined previously. This will be somebody whom you neither like nor dislike strongly. At first you may not have any great feelings at all. Try to stay, however, with whatever feelings actually come to the surface. Work on improving those bland feelings in a positive direction insofar as you can. Ask for good things to happen to that person. When you are ready, turn your attention towards another person whom, in your opinion, you do not get on well with at all – a person who grates on you or someone who irritates you to a degree. Someone you dislike or who seems to think little of you. Become aware of the feelings that seem to well up in you as you bring them to the forefront of your imagination. You will probably make assumptions about how you think you will feel when their image comes into your imagination but stay with the feelings that actually emerge. Insofar as you can, try to let go of any feelings of acrimony and animosity that rise like bile to your mouth. Such feelings are much more likely to do you damage than the person they are directed towards.

For the final stage of this meditation, try to situate all four characters (yourself, your good friend, the neutral person and the loathsome individual) together into a group in your imagination. Your feelings and wishes for your friend will be warm and generous but try to conjure up good for the others too. Pray that the Lord will look favourably towards them all and gift them with His grace. Ask that good may come to the despised one as much as it may come to your good friend. Keep this up for some little time.

When you are ready, gradually bring the meditation to an end. Don't bring the proceedings to an end too abruptly, as this may jar your mood and leave you with an unpleasant feeling. Give yourself a few minutes quiet – an oasis of peace, as it were. Sometimes the fruit of such a meditation may take some little time to sink in and you may have to work assiduously to find out how it has affected you.

CHAPTER 9

DEALING WITH DEATH

Do not wait for the last judgement. It takes place every day.

– Albert Camus

In the east, they tell a cautionary tale. It concerns a master who sent his servant to the market-place to buy provisions. Some little time afterwards the servant returned home, looking both pale and worried. When asked what the matter was, he replied that he had met a horrible stranger along his route. The fellow was the very image of death itself. Worse still, the stranger seemed to know who he was and was keen to cement their acquaintance. The poor servant begged his master to lend him a fast horse so that he could put as much distance between himself and the figure of death as possible, for he felt that if he could get himself away from his present location he might be able to avoid death's grasp. The generous master did as he was asked and supplied the horse and thus the servant departed. Some time later, the master himself had occasion to visit the same market-place and was surprised to find the figure of death still hovering around. Annoyed, he challenged death head-on and asked it why it had given his servant such a threatening look. 'Why, that wasn't a threatening look,' death replied, 'it was a look of surprise. I never expected to see your servant here. In fact, I have an appointment with him this very evening – but in a place many miles from here.'

We all have an appointment with death. It's one of the few things we can be certain about. It's interesting to see how many of us push this fact as far into the background as we can. In everyday life, signs that our expiry date is approaching are constantly rearing their head. We can see them, if we care to look, in physical change, diminished eyesight, greying hair, flabby body, and loss of energy, not to mention a general slowing down in our metabolism. Various body parts begin to give out, signifying the approach of death, but we go blithely on, burying our head in the sand. We don't anticipate, we don't plan, and we don't change.

A different kind of death also may be approaching and it's not such an obvious one. It's a type of death that eats away from the inside and it is best illustrated by an unusual jellyfish they have in Naples. These jellyfish are surrounded by danger, even though they don't know it themselves. The danger lies in a category of food that lies all around – a local variety of snail. It has a particularly hard shell. If a jellyfish eats one of the snails, damage begins. It cannot digest the shell part of the snail. Worse still, as soon as it is ingested, the tiny snail begins to eat the jellyfish from the inside. Unless the jellyfish manages to vomit up the snail, the tiny creature inside will eventually lead to its doom and destruction. It consumes and damages from within.

Throughout life, events and situations are constantly taking place around us. Some seem like they will be to our benefit. Others are less healthy. But whether these events will bring us life or death, glory or disgrace, who can tell?

Quite recently, a study was conducted in England to see how 17-year-old girls were faring in society at present. It seemed to those carrying out the research that opportunities for girls of this age-bracket had never been brighter. Greater numbers than ever were remaining on at school and girls now outnumbered boys and were doing better academically than their male counterparts. Everything in the garden seemed rosy. The results revealed, however, that such suppositions were false. What appeared beneficial had a downside. The ground-breaking study by Patrick West and Helen Sweeting of Glasgow University showed that an alarming new trend was manifesting itself among upper-class teenage girls in the London area. It indicated that they constantly feel anxious and depressed. Compared with only 16 years ago, young girls are dramatically – worryingly – more miserable. West measured levels of anxiety and depression in two large, representative samples in 1987 and again in 1999. Among the working classes, there wasn't much difference in the levels of stress he encountered, but, in the top economic groupings, the rise in stress levels had rocketed. As the report put it, the teenage girls were from 24 per cent to 38 per cent unhappier than heretofore. Surprisingly, during the time-frame chosen, there was no increase in unhappiness among young males in any economic group though it is hard to say precisely why. Perhaps the boys had stepped out of the competitive milieu. In any event, the girls now felt very driven. They felt they had to succeed and were desperate to please. These factors created stress as well as self-hatred. What had seemed like a blessing – emancipation – had turned out to be less than what they had supposed or hoped for. To regain their equilibrium, change would be required.

The time for such change is not when our powers have diminished, our resolve weakened, our spirits demoralised and our hopes faded, but rather while we are still flexible. This fact is shown to us even in nature. The wolf spider, for example, does not allow itself to become rigid or stubborn. It does not build its web between two solid objects such as rocks. It knows that when the wind blows – as ill winds will sometimes blow in insect lives as well as human ones – being stuck in such a rigid position would mean disaster. The web would be demolished. Instead, it chooses to spin its web between two movable objects such as blades of grass. That way, when the going gets tough and the winds howl, the web will be able to bend. When better times return, it can regain its former shape. We can learn something from its example.

Look towards Christ as a model. He regularly turned His face towards the future and spoke with His disciples about what might happen to Him. Whatever about preparing Himself, He certainly tried to prepare them for any eventuality. He knew that the time to prepare was while they still had their Saviour with them, and while they were, in a manner of speaking, still in robust health. It would be too late to start renewal when He had been removed from their midst. His removal, unless prepared for, would take with it what they most desperately required – the enthusiasm and courage to go on. Christ knew that the time to plan was while they were still on top, still vibrant, still empowered.

Even when we're not on top, however, we can still make strides forward. The famous Hollywood director, Cecil B. de Mille tells a story about being on holiday in Northern Maine. It was a lazy sort of vacation and he spent much of the time in a canoe on the water. As he drifted about, he noticed a swarm of beetles that had settled on the water, close to his canoe. One of these insects crawled on his craft and stuck its legs into the wood. Then it died. The film director says he returned to the reading of his book but after about three hours he happened to look down. The beetle was still there and had dried up, but, as he watched, something happened. Its back split open and a miracle began. First a head, then wings, then a whole new body began to make itself visible. New creation was beginning. In a phoenix-like manner, new life was beginning to emerge from the body of the dead beetle. In fact, a beautiful dragonfly was coming forth. De Mille commented that what looked like a tomb had been – in a sense – a womb for new life.

It would have been easy for de Mille to see only the death scene. In fact he did not. He didn't allow the sense of approaching death to block out the possibility of something wonderful and new emerging. That is unusual. You may have heard of a man called Elie Wiesel. He was liberated from Buchenwald concentration camp in 1945 and says that his time there was one long, living nightmare. Living through such a horrendous experience, he says, quenched the very faith in his soul. It's not easy to keep out the darkness and it's even more difficult to see silver linings when so many black clouds abound.

Having some sense of God's presence in our lives during times of trouble is a tremendous gift. Occasionally God will grant us that favour. When this happens, be extremely grateful. If the gift is not offered, remember the old Irish prayer: 'If you can keep a green branch alive in your heart during the hours of darkness, then the Lord will come and send a bird to sing from that branch at the dawning of the day'. Wait for the dawn. Do not let the darkness go unchallenged for that is what allows evil to flourish.

As Martin Niemöller famously pointed out, allowing wickedness to go uncontested is exactly what produced the horror of Germany during the Nazi era. Many did not confront darkness while they still had the chance. Buber himself, while he had still influence, did not do enough. He saw signs of evil rising like an evil tide around him but failed to oppose Hitler's regime. When he finally decided to do something, it was too late. In a famous statement he says, 'When Hitler attacked the Jews I was not concerned, for I was not a Jew. When he attacked the Catholics, I still stood to one side, for I was not a Catholic. When he attacked the unions and the industrialists, I held my peace for I was not a union member. I was not concerned. Finally Hitler attacked me, and the Protestant Church. By that stage, there was nobody left to be concerned.'

We should attack darkness and despair whether they come from within or without. It's a mistake to think that the elements of despair always come from without. Sometimes we can manufacture them from within. Trapped rattlesnakes are known to occasionally become so angry and frustrated that they bite themselves. Human beings at times display the same harmful tendencies. When they lose the run of themselves they become vindictive and poisonous and end up destroying themselves.

Attack evil, even if the task seems impossible. Take heart from the example of Alice and the queen as revealed by Lewis Carroll. When confronted with a huge dilemma, Alice laughs and says, 'There's no use trying – one can't believe impossible things.' The queen replied, 'I dare say you haven't had much practice. When I was your age, I always did it for half an hour each day. Why, sometimes, I've believed as many as six impossible things before breakfast.'

To retain hope and belief in the impossible, keep your eye on Jesus. In one American Indian tribe an old chief was asked why he believed so much in the person of Jesus and why he was always making silent incan-tations to Him. The chief didn't say anything for a while. Then he col-lected some dried grass and twigs and arranged them in a circle. Next he picked up a caterpillar, feeding on a nearby clump of trees. He placed the caterpillar inside the circle after which he took a match and set fire to the grass and twigs. As the fire blazed up, the caterpillar searched for a way out of his dilemma. Just when it looked as though all hope was lost and no means of escape could be found, the old chief extended his finger to the caterpillar. The insect hopped on to it. The Indian chief quietly told those around him, 'That's what Jesus did for me. In my youth I was like the caterpillar – confused, threatened, and without hope. I know at some point Jesus stretched out his hand towards me and I grabbed hold of it. He rescued me.'

Some might accuse the Indian chief of living in the Dark Ages. In fact that's exactly what he refused to do. He knew that an age is called dark, not because the light fails to shine but, because people ignore the possibility of light beginning to shine on their affairs. Feed your faith in whatever way possible, and your doubts will begin to starve themselves to death. It's never easy.

Fr Peter McVerry should know a thing or two about facing dark clouds. He's an Irish Jesuit and is well known for working with the home-less and hopeless. About his own prayer he says, 'The prayer of despera-tion taught me to face my own humanity and helplessness and let God be God. It is His Kingdom we are building, not our own. He knows what He is doing. He is still in charge, the Master Architect, I hope. It is His children who are dying, who are suffering and He has His reasons. I don't know what they are. If I did, I would be God.'

So travel on towards the end with a touch of that courage. Do not allow any darkness that went before hold you back. It's how our lives end that should be uppermost in our minds now. I like a *Peanuts* cartoon that may give us courage here. It shows Lucy holding a music box up to her ear and listening attentively. After a few seconds she turns to Charlie Brown and explains, 'I always like to begin my day listening to good mu-sic.' Charlie is obviously confused, and unimpressed. In his reply he says, 'I'm not concerned with how my day begins. It's how it ends that bothers me.'

*

Exercise One
Inner Peace

Take time out and go to a quiet, safe place. Seat yourself on a straight-backed chair and quietly breathe in and out. Become aware of the point of contact between your body and the chair and note how the chair supports your body. As you breathe in, note the cool air as it fills your insides and allow the action of the incoming air to calm you. As you breathe out, allow any tension within your stomach area to dissipate.

Imagine going deeper and deeper inside yourself until you come to a place of rest and peace within. This is a region where the cares of the world seem far away. Take a moment to simply let yourself be in this peaceful place where there is absolutely nothing you have to do. In this quiet place within, you are close to your deepest wisdom – that is, you are close to the part of you that is insightful and wise and knows what you need. In meditation, it is often believed that the subconscious acts as an 'inner guide' or 'guardian angel'.

Our inner guide often points out that 'rushing about and doing things', even if it at first seems satisfying, can often be a substitute for more important work for we need, at regular intervals, to sit down and take a good look at what is going on inside.

The subconscious or 'inner guide' may help discern what distress or unhappiness is prompting your action in the first place. If – during this meditation – you have questions you want to throw at your inner guide, go ahead. Try to be open so that you may receive what that 'wisest' part of yourself may be offering.

*

Exercise Two
Praying in Secret

First read the text from chapter 6, verses 5–7, from St Matthew's Gospel:

> When you pray, do not imitate the hypocrites: they love to say their prayers standing up in the synagogues and at the street corners for people to see them. In truth, I tell you, they have had their reward. But when you pray, go to your private room, shut yourself in and so pray to your Father who is in that secret place and your Father who sees all that is done in secret will reward you.

Go to a quiet place where you feel safe. You want to be quiet with Jesus for a while. Place yourself in a sitting posture with your back straight and your hands placed in your lap. Begin to notice your breathing pattern as you draw the air gently through your nostril and down into your stomach. After a few moments, allow the air to depart from your body, beginning deep down in your stomach and visualising it as it works its way up along your backbone, into your chest cavity, up into your throat and out your mouth. Usually a few minutes of this regular paced breathing in and out brings with it a sense of peace and relaxation though it is not absolutely necessary to feel the relaxation for it to have a beneficial effect. Sometimes you may be bombarded with thousands of thoughts or distractions. Be gentle with yourself. Try to work creatively to find ways of making your practice as comfortable as you can and stay in the present moment. Much of our stress comes from thinking about past or future worries – often things you can do little about. When you manage to focus on what you are doing at the present moment there is little room for any other subject matter to make itself felt. If you find yourself straying towards worries of the past, or fears for the future, draw your attention gently back to the present. Think of the distractions as objects and say to them: 'Now I am having a distraction. I will move it over to a imaginary shelf in my mind and get back to the business at hand.'

I begin now to think about how Jesus prayed and how He advised others to develop the practice of prayer for themselves. Even a cursory look at Jesus' life shows He took time out regularly to be by Himself so that He could commune with the Father. That's what He told His disciples to do also. Is He inviting me to do the same? Each time Jesus carved out moments of profound silence for Himself, He first reminded Himself that His Father was very near. That might be my starting point also: 'Father, I have come here today because I want to let Your presence fill me and even though at times I do not feel You close, I know You understand me better than I do myself. I have come here to sit for a few moments so that I can share with You what has been going on in my life. Sometimes it feels like I am just speaking into the darkness but in my better moments I sense Your closeness quite clearly and now I beg for a sense of that affinity to strengthen my belief. I know that You can create order out of chaos and make good sense out of nonsense. You did it for Your Son and so I take my courage in my hands and ask You to do it also for me.'

*

EXERCISE THREE
Martha and Mary
[St Luke's Gospel 10:38–42]

The story of Martha and Mary in the Gospels can be re-visited time and time again. You will usually find something different in it to dwell upon each time:

> As Jesus and His disciples were on their way, He entered a village and a woman called Martha welcomed Him to her house. She had a sister named Mary who sat down at the Lord's feet to listen to His words. Martha, meanwhile, was busy with all the serving and finally she said, 'Lord, don't you care that my sister has left me to do all the serving?' But the Lord answered, 'Martha, Martha, you worry and are troubled about many things whereas only one thing is needed. Mary has chosen the better part and it will not be taken from her'.

Take up one of the usual meditation postures and relax into a comfortable position.

Pay attention to how your body is, starting with how you feel and any sensations you may be experiencing. Now turn your awareness to the top of your head and your face.

Can you feel any tingling in that area? Take your time before bringing your attention down to your shoulders. Watch for tautness because tension is often stored there. Try to stay loose and when you are ready, draw the focus of your attention down to your chest area. Check to see if it is relaxed. Now move your awareness downward and check out the trunk of your body. Just be aware of how it is before you move your observance to your legs and then your feet, noting that they are the points of contact with the chair and floor.

At first you are simply trying to be aware of how you and the different parts of your body are. Take as much time as you like and when you feel ready – proceed.

First read the story of Martha and Mary and just try to get into the scene. Note how Martha is at home in her house working flat out. So much to do, and so little time. That feels a little bit like myself really. Observe as Martha hears sounds outside her house and recognises the voice of Jesus. Conflicting emotions overtake her. Jesus is a friend whom she knows and likes greatly and on any other day she would be honoured and delighted if He decided to visit. But why has He chosen today of all days when she finds herself incredible busy? As soon as Jesus enters the house He can sense her unease. Could it be that He picks up the same vibes when He comes to visit me? 'Go away and come back at a more opportune time' may also be my signature tune.

I imagine myself as Martha. Just then, my sister Mary enters the scene. Without apology, she finds a place beside Jesus and opens a conversation. I can feel a rush of envy and anger. Envy over her easy ability to just be with Jesus and anger over the way she has so lightly skipped out of her share of the housework and left the lot to me. Somewhere deep down I am aware of feelings of resentment and sadness tugging me in two directions. Work calls, and I am resentful to be left with more than my fair share of it. Sadness too, because I recognise an opportunity to be present with and interact with Jesus. So in a sense of pique I ask Jesus to intervene on my behalf and make my sister shoulder her share of the family responsibilities. I'm rather surprised at His reply. My sister has chosen the better part, I'm told. I did not have to isolate myself in the kitchen. No one forced me into that role. I could have carved out the time and stayed at His feet, but I didn't.

I decide to make a special prayer. Lord, help me to go slower and enjoy life. Help me not to be always running and not to always have a list of engagements that prevent me enjoying your presence. Teach me not to be a victim to my own compulsions. Help me to 'do' less and to 'be' more. When I am ready I bring the meditation to a close.

*

Exercise Four
Nicodemus
[St John's Gospel 3:1–15]

As you start a meditation, it is useful to have some idea about its theme. Try to work out what grace or wisdom you are seeking. In this case, I ask for courage and the ability to act in an honest way.

Begin by sitting quietly for a minute or two. Relax, and settle down. Now turn your attention to the following passage:

> Among the Pharisees there was a ruler named Nicodemus. He came to Jesus at night and said, 'Rabbi, we know that you have come from God to teach us, for no one can perform miracles like yours unless God is with them'. Jesus replied, 'Truly I say to you, no one can see the kingdom of God unless he is born again from above'. Nicodemus said, 'How can there be rebirth for a grown man? Who could go back to his mothers womb and be born again?'

Jesus replied, 'Truly I say to you, unless one is born again of water and the Spirit, he cannot enter the kingdom of God. What is born of the flesh, is flesh. And what is born of the Spirit, is Spirit. Because of this, do not be surprised when I say, you must be born again from above'.

Think about Nicodemus. We are told that this man was a leader of his people and must therefore have regularly heard about Jesus, a new 'guru' who had come to his area. While others were threatened and disturbed by the news, Nicodemus was enthralled. He knew that he wanted and needed to meet this astounding individual. Instead of keeping these wishes dormant, Nicodemus made it his business to search out Jesus for himself. So many others were finding hope and life in this new guru that Nicodemus felt that he himself, at the very least, should discover more. What was all the excitement about? Being a leader, he did possess prudence and waited until dark before he sought Jesus out for there was little point in ruining his own reputation if Jesus turned out to be an imposter.

In your imagination, go with Nicodemus now as he makes his way to an unfamiliar area of town for this is where he has heard Jesus was most likely to be found. Watch him as he makes his way warily along, casting the occasional glance back over his shoulder to make sure he is not being followed. Note how he pulls his cloak over his head to disguise his identity as much as possible. Listen as he mutters to himself and questions his own sanity at the task he is about to perform. Often enough he has to hide both his thoughts and feelings even to himself. Deep down he knows that he is not truly happy. There's a sort of restlessness inside. He's in search of something – but what that 'something' is he knows not.

Keep your eyes locked on Nicodemus as he asks bystanders if they know where Jesus might be staying. Finally, one answers in the affirmative. Nicodemus follows the directions he's given. Stay with him as he spots Jesus and makes his way over to Him. Watch the surprise on Jesus' face as He sees who has come to visit Him. Visits from such dignitaries are rare. Usually such holders of powerful positions are His enemy. But this one seems different. Watch Jesus listening to Nicodemus. Note how he ponders his questions and frames suitable replies in His mind. You are a little distance away so you can hardly hear their shared conversation. At length you can just make out Jesus expressing His thanks to Nicodemus for the risk he has taken. You may also hear Him tell Nicodemus that his world isolates him from the experience, sufferings and pain of the poor. It's difficult for Nicodemus to feel the common people's pain but you can see that a realisation is slowly coming to him that the path ahead will not be easy. If he can achieve at least part of the challenge that is being put before him however, perhaps great inner life might result. 'Nicodemus, how far are you prepared to put yourself out for those around you?' Watch his panic as he realises the implications of the question put to him. He is being asked to leave his comfortable existence and step out in a new direction.

Suddenly Jesus turns His gaze away from Nicodemus and towards you. Hear the question coming from Jesus' mouth in your direction: 'And you – would also like to be born again?' I try to ponder for myself what that question might demand of me. Might I need to refocus and look at those around me and see what their needs are? Do I want to be born again? Only I can give an honest answer to that question.

CHAPTER 10

THE IRISH CHURCH GROWING UP

It is the duty of the ship's captain to make port, cost what it may
— Antoine de Saint-Exupéry

Growing up is always hard. It's as hard in the faith area as it is in any other and in Ireland, where the winds of change have blown with remarkable rapidity in recent times, the need for Christians to look at their faith, beliefs and practice is almost obligatory. If they do not, those self-same winds of change will demolish them, for the religious voice, which up to now had been insistent and strong, is no longer the player it once was and perhaps is hardly a player at all. At least that's the way it seems to me right now and it's also the way things appeared to Henri Nouwen when his native Holland underwent a similarly cataclysmic shake-up to their long held beliefs some years ago. He mentions in his writings that he was flabbergasted at how quickly a society could alter its values and how quickly its people could be asked to change and grow. It seemed to him that Holland had moved from being a very pious to a very secular country in a remarkable short space of time. This knocked many out of alignment and vast numbers of its people had to first find their new bearings and then readjust themselves to their new situation accordingly.

Nouwen's observations about how faith practices and beliefs were shaken to their core in his native Holland some years ago seem to resonate in many respects with Ireland's situation today. That our culture and lifestyle have changed is undeniable but the effect of those changes on our inner spirit has been less easy to quantify. Social scientists grapple for reasons for this change and a number of theories are offered. People are busy – very busy. Many of the population seem like rowers in a boat-race and we get the impression that if they do not row forward frantically, then – at least in their own minds – they run the risk of not only remaining static but of actually being carried backwards.

The frantic paddling we are engaged in means we have little time to reflect on where our paddling is leading us or what the pace of life may be doing to our inner peace. This trend, it seems to me, seems particularly prevalent among our younger people, for in schools, universities and third-level institutions, students appear to work harder and harder just to keep up with the herd. Their lifestyle demands that they add to their burden by taking on part-time employment so that whatever leisure time they do possess gets filled with more and more activity.

It has to be admitted that all this has an upside, but – it seems to me – a downside exists also, which is not much commented upon. It makes them more competitive in the market-place but more driven and fatigued in spirit. It means that, for them, God may well be missing – but not missed.

The 'fast-track' approach to success in life is not the only factor that appears to be effecting change. A second ingredient seems to have emerged in Ireland today. Old authorities – not to mention authority figures – have been having a hard time and no longer hold the sway they once did. Cherished institutions of yesteryear that were looked up to and revered no longer receive that veneration. They are seen to have feet of clay and are often accused of being authority-ridden and paternal. Religious institutions – though I may be shouldering a bit of a bias here – have received a heavier hammering than most in this regard and their demise has been rapid and startling. 'Alleluia!', some say, because they have aided and abetted their own downfall by misdemeanour and intrigue. Too much power tends to be corroding and corrupting and thus a part of me joins in the 'Alleluia' myself. The more cautionary part however, is uneasy. It remembers that in our noviceship house we had a lake. It seems that years ago bits of weed grew at the bottom of this lake which caused a certain amount of annoyance. Some bright spark had the idea of introducing a foreign plant of some kind that was supposed to eradicate the original weed. In fact what happened was that the new monstrosity supplanted the old, taking over the whole lake and causing an almighty mess. In essence, what sprang up as the supposed solution was much worse than the original difficulty.

So it may be with our faith practices in Ireland today. A vacuum has been created but such a void does not remain empty for very long. Into the gap a new set of values is already beginning to make its way where moral guidelines, not to mention wise words of wisdom handed down from generation to generation, are now being given very scant regard. A sort of moral 'wooziness' is becoming the order of the day where objective standards seem hard to come by and a sort of 'a la carte' philosophy

– without any effective counter-balance – has spread its influence unchecked.

Individual freedom is highly valued today and this certainly has an attractive side to it. What's not so obvious is its downside. Nothing seems to be obviously right or wrong and the vagueness and confusion that engenders saps energy. This leaves many with a dilemma. How should we stand firm and talk about God from within the walls of a discredited Church? How can we combat the sense of perplexity and desolation that appears to have filtered into so many young hearts? Pope Paul VI put it well, 'The split between the Gospel and culture is without doubt the tragedy of our time'. Our culture has been under pressure and our lifestyle has changed at a phenomenal pace. Discerning and committed Christians have the right and the duty to ask themselves and anyone else who will listen – has the growth been a case of growing up, or growing ill?

Brendan Kennelly, the Irish poet, has pertinent observations to make on this point, as has Carl Jung, the famous Swiss psychologist. Both have noticed a trend in our culture and it's to do with things moving too quickly. Jung said that 'Hurry is not of the devil but it is the devil' while Kennelly observed that in modern Ireland nobody seems to have time to see what is really going on around him or her any more. They do not even have time to look at themselves. Haste, hurry, stress, and pressure seem to be the new gods to them and this fact sits very uneasily with the poet in Kennelly who feels inspired, and maybe even compelled, to stand back and survey our times and milieu. Particularly in moments of frenetic activity, the necessity for paying more urgent attention to what is going on 'within' is all the greater, he feels. As we seek relief from our busyness, we end up further exhausting ourselves with over-stimulating activity. Perhaps we avoid quiet because it scares us. Maybe we fear that once we're quiet and vulnerable, the terrible reality might dawn on us that life is, after all, meaningless. Our own poverty of spirit may keep us hurrying toward spiritual death.

In earlier ages, Pascal and Pythagoras found themselves having to contend with similar stark realities and hinted that there is tremendous value to be had from creating inner space for ourselves. It helps us distinguish between urgent and important things. If we allow only what is urgent to dominate our day, we will never get around to what is truly important and the result will be a growing sense of dissatisfaction. Some of the best spiritual directors have pointed out that urgent things regularly surround us and these have a habit of distracting us from facing what is really important unless we are careful. Creating adult faith is what we are about here but a good deal of frustration will be our lot if we do not carve out periods of reflection and silence to look long and steadily, sifting though what might be valuable along the road ahead. The modern disease we run the risk of catching is a sort of post modern 'whatever you're having yourself' type of lifestyle.

Some have coined the term 'New Age' to describe it and it's particularly attractive to those who abhor the strictures and dogmas of organised religion. It's becoming more and more usual in Ireland today to hear people describing themselves as 'spiritual' rather than as a believer in any one religion. As I understand it, the best of this new thinking seeks to learn and enrich itself by becoming open to the riches of other cultures.

The worst of 'New Age', however, goes down a different path. It appears to mix and match odds and ends from all religions – as well as none – and seems particularly interested in eastern religions and cults. It paints itself as 'spiritual' but it is spirituality without church, sin or judgement. It has an appeal for some younger people because it seems to free them from formal and institutionalised religious set-ups. Older Christians have their doubts, however. They see their younger counterparts galloping around grabbing at any new fad that raises its head and the elders are bemused, wondering how people can throw away riches that are tried and tested. Experience has taught the elders that the soul needs wholesome food and their experience of life has pointed them in directions where nourishing fare might be unearthed.

To check, as we grow older, whether our faith practice is still providing nutritious fare, we might keep a journal or diary to make the link between our outer journey and our inner journey. When I speak of such a journal, I have in mind a notebook or 'diary of the emotions', in which people jot down the patterns they are discovering within themselves, as well as any feelings, consolations, desolations, highs and lows that seem to be making appearances within their orbit. If the new data wakes them up in a way that discommodes them, it may prove to be beneficial for they will have to do something about it. At the very least it will force them to grow closer to their own vulnerability and will sharpen the practice of recognising what is going on within. People know that they are going to encounter new experiences in their lives on a regular basis and if they are wise they won't want to miss the meaning of what these events might mean.

Pause for a moment and allow your memory to rove over proceedings that have overtaken you during the last few months. These may have been meetings with friends, conversations with enemies, or even adventures which happened to others but which you witnessed. The first thing about taking jottings on these proceedings is that you mark the incident in your mind and become conscious of it. So first you ask yourself, 'What happened?' Now, in the journal, register for yourself whether you reflected on the episode or not. Did you just let it pass by unnoticed or did you try to pray about what the incident might be saying to you?

One good reason for keeping a journal is that if God speaks to us He'd prefer not to have to use a megaphone. Throughout the Old Testament the suggestion seems to be that God is actively seeking to communicate from His side and any co-operation that we can provide would be deeply appreciated. The journal and its jottings give substance to such questions as: What happened to me recently? Why did it happen? How did I respond to the incident? What lessons has that episode for me? Reflecting on what happened, why it happened, and what feelings it dredged up within me may well alter the way I react to similar situations in the future. If we are lucky, the meaning of the incidence may be clear at the moment we have the experience.

On other occasions, and perhaps more commonly, the best interpretation and analysis will only be apparent with hindsight. We may, as it were, need to hold up a mirror to see what's going on and what it means. Other people – along with their insights and comments – can be that mirror for their wisdom illustrates for us facets of ourselves that we had not hitherto understood. The jottings that we keep in the journal – allied with the dialogue that we undertake with God, others or ourselves – help unravel the mystery that we sometimes are to ourselves. By using the journal regularly we gain greater insight into feelings, emotions, reactions, and reflections that we observe in ourselves concerning the event under scrutiny.

It's helpful to record notes reasonably close to the time the event occurs, as delay distorts the memory and put layers of questionable interpretation on the proceedings. You may well be surprised with what you discover and your findings will probably shape the way you tackle upcoming events. Even though you may think you know what is in the pipeline for you in the immediate future, you may be remarkably wide of the mark.

Anthony de Mello used to tell a story about a Rabbi who planned his future pretty carefully and who ran his life like clockwork. He was so settled in his behaviour that his friends used to say that he could have written his own life story even before the events unfolded. The Rabbi insisted this was completely untrue. He illustrated how unpredictable things can be that very same day for, as he made his way to the synagogue he was approached by local police who asked him where he was going. ' I don't know', the honest Rabbi replied, even though he seldom altered his route or his prayer practice from day to day. He was immediately thrown into jail for being evasive. When afterwards, this charge was read out to him in court and the prosecutor said that, as he never varied his routine, he must have known where he was going, the Rabbi replied, 'Well look where I am now. As you can see I didn't know where I was going, nor, for that matter, did I know where I would end up.'

So, wise people move towards the future holding on to their faith as best they can, trying to improve on it, even if the time of their approaching end is uncertain, and their beliefs are regularly put to the test. Keeping faith in what they were given and remaining loyal to their heritage is not always easy. One father found this out for himself a couple of years ago in Armenia, where an earthquake struck his village and the catastrophe killed 30,000 people. Among them, it seemed, was his son. The boy had left home that morning for his school and the building, according to reports, had been flattened. The devastated father rushed to the spot as quickly as he could and, upon arrival, found things more or less as he had been told. Remembering that his son's classroom was at the back of the school, he straightaway began digging there.

Hour after hour he continued his search, even though those around him told him that no one could possibly have survived for so long. After 38 hours, the father finally heard a faint whimpering. It was his son. Amazingly, a tiny space had formed itself within the rubble, allowing the small boy, and a few friends, to survive. Afterwards, when the young lad was telling his story, he recounted how his father often mentioned that faith – including his own – would often be put to the test. That day it was. The boys who were buried alive around him doubted that any of them would ever be located but he, despite reservations, insisted they had nothing to fear. Down in the darkness he maintained to any who would listen that he was absolutely certain his father would come. That conviction, uttered with more confidence than was justified, kept him going. It also gave courage to the others.

Such faith – or lack of it – is a gift. It's not something we have by right but it is something we can pray for or ask to be led towards by others. Some people have a particular gift of bestowing it on those around them. General Dwight D. Eisenhower, who was commander of the Allied forces during the Second World War, seemed to have the effect on his troops and staff. To those who would listen, he suggested way of imbuing others with confidence and illustrated his point by taking a piece of string and putting it down on a table. To those listening he pointed out that, if you pull or draw this string gently but firmly, it will follow you in any direction you care to go. If, on the other hand, you attempt to push or shove the string, it will snarl up and go in all directions. It's the same with people. Draw or pull them with kindness and encouragement towards growth and they will go in your direction. Attempt to push or shove them, however, and they will dig in and resist you mightily. The growth we are looking for in our own faith is towards life and vibrancy. Growth, however, as we know only too well, can either be positive or poisonous. The growth we are trying to avoid is one that can creep up on us, cancer-like, as a disease.

Within the Irish Church, growth – whether of a positive or poisonous nature – has been on the agenda for some time now. It has been forced upon us whether we like it or not. Many within the Church feel like the threatened moth that botanists study. They illustrate this by speaking of a man who went out for a stroll. As he walked, he came upon a moth, ensconced inside a cocoon, and attached to the branch of a tree. The passer-by took the whole branch home, not wanting to disturb the tiny creature inside. Days passed, and, as far as the walker could see, there was little or no movement inside the cocoon. This disappointed the passer-by, and thinking he might help nature along, he slit the cocoon along one side, making it easier for the moth to appear, which indeed it did, in double-quick time. Unfortunately, it appeared before its natural time and emerged deformed. The botanists explain, when they tell the story, that nature has its own pace and its own challenge. The moth needs to struggle free from its abode if it is to grow strong and healthy. The very act of forcing itself out of the cocoon strengthens its wings. By splitting the cocoon the stranger helped the moth in its task but it also meant that it could not prepare itself for its destiny.

We must prepare ourselves for ours, just as the desert fathers did so many years ago when they made their way forward through many perils. Not all survived and some abandoned the struggle. When asked why not all remained true to their calling, one old abbot explained that monastic life is a life of pursuit – searching for God. It's as if a dog were chasing a hare, running after it, yelping and barking. This excitement is contagious and causes others to join in the chase. After a time all those who do not see the hare for themselves grow tired. One after another they drop out.

The monk finished by saying that only those who keep their eyes on the crucified Lord persevere to the end.

*

EXERCISE ONE
Joseph and Mary as Teachers
[Luke 2:39]

First read the passage from chapter 2, verse 39 of St Luke's Gospel:

> They went back to Galilee, to their own town of Nazareth. And as the child grew to maturity, he was filled with wisdom and God's favour was with him.

Start by taking a number of deep, refreshing breaths. Remember that you can even use your breathing as a form of prayer. God, we are told, first gave and encouraged life by breathing into the first thing He created and so it may help to remind yourself that each gulp of air you take is something to be grateful for and a gift from God. As soon as you feel settled, begin.

Go, in your imagination, to the place Jesus Himself grew up in. You have to paint this place in your mind's eye but for many it will probably be a simple place – and a restful one too. Now sketch in for yourself a picture of Jesus as a boy of about 12 years of age and let Him begin to tell you about what being a child was like for Him. He may begin by talking about His parents – His earthly ones, that is. First, He might begin to tell you stories about His mother. What aspect of her character or goodness does He concentrate on? After this, Jesus may move on to speak about Joseph who was a quiet man, honest and determined, passing on the skills necessary to carve out a living. Let Him speak about His happiest memories and then respond if He asks you to recount your own childhood. You might begin like He did, mentioning special moments or unique people you cannot forget. Perhaps you might even take Him, in your imagination, to the house you grew up in and recount events or individual you particularly remember.

He may ask about your own parents – so introduce Him to your mother or father or both. Happy events may come to the surface first, but difficult moments may make an appearance as well. If He laughs and speaks about the time He managed to get Himself lost and thereby upset His parents – that might give you an opening. Just as He worried His parents dreadfully, you might recall a time when something less than perfect happened between yourself and either your own mother or father. Think back to any incident that produced tension and strife. Maybe you said things you really didn't mean, or acted in a way that that now brings back remorse and shame. That may prompt Jesus to tell you about the time His family went to Jerusalem. He will explain somewhat ruefully how He managed to get Himself left behind in the temple. Not, He will admit, one of His better moments. He will paint for you the picture of how tears and recriminations flowed when His parents finally discovered Him. How He tried to explain what had happened, but felt that – for once – He was not being listened to. And all this even though He believed He was doing His Father's will. He will recall for you how Joseph and Mary were more upset than He had ever seen them. Most unusually, they seemed frightening and forbidding. The atmosphere that had been created wasn't His fault and wasn't intentional, but as He talks to you He remembers it still – and it hasn't lost its power to bring both recrimination and hurt.

As the two of you go down memory lane, the mood brightens. You both begin to recall happier moments when you knew you were loved. When the warmth of your parent's goodness brought out all your richness and gifts. Now take a little time to give thanks for those moments and the people who produced them. Give thanks also for the confidence and sense of security they subsequently brought you and gently finish the meditation.

*

Exercise Two
Does Jesus Speak to Me?

You may have heard something about Ignatian spirituality. The concept and terminology is linked to the thinking and praying habits of St Ignatius of Loyola and tries to spell out how Ignatius taught others to pray. A central tenet is that God made us to be with Him forever and continually tries to develop a bond with us towards that end. That bonding, it seems, entails His speaking to us. I've always had trouble with that last part. I suppose I'm a bit of a dull fellow but I never knew what it meant. If the concept is true, I always wanted to know when, exactly, where and how He does His speaking – I seem to hear so little! He sometimes seems remarkably absent from my world. So where is this God – that Ignatian spirituality tells me is communicating and conversing with me – being so proactive?

I may have been given my answer very recently. I was asked to conduct an Advent evening of prayer in one of the toughest parishes in Dublin and as I made my way out to their small and heavily guarded church I have to admit that the main concern on my mind was not what you might expect. Instead of wondering how the evening might go, or whether the parishioners would find anything spiritually nourishing during the session, I found myself fretting over where I might park my motorbike. My main anxiety was that my means of transport might be spirited away.

Well, I have to report that the people were lovely, and particularly warm-hearted, and at the end one of them came up quietly and told me that the day had been the worst of her life. Everything about her life had reached an all-time low. As she put it herself, 'Things were so bad that if a train had come along and run over me, I would have considered that it was doing me a favour'. She had no idea what had drawn her to the church that evening. Something just seemed to suggest it. 'It was pure wonderful,' she said. 'As we got into the meditation I could just feel my spirits lifting and the gloom began to lift itself from my shoulders.' Then she hit me with her clincher. 'I think God must have sent you along specially.' Now I have to tell you that the last thing I felt like was that God had done any such thing. A hundred and ten other things might have been going through my head, but the thought that I was a special ambassador from God wasn't on the radar screen at all.

But who told St Paul that he was God's emissary? Did some of the saints know any better than we that they were the Almighty's representatives, sent to be His presence to those around them? I think not. When we are told that God speaks to us, isn't it more than likely that He uses you and me to make His words and actions become a reality? As I came home on the bike that evening, the very thought took my breath away.

Begin the meditation in the usual way. Now prepare.

Be with Jesus in your imagination. He will let you see that you are His joy and delight. Close your eyes and relax. As you breathe in and out try to be aware of the life you are drawing in to yourself. Now take time off in a favourite place of yours where you will feel safe with Jesus. Note how He takes a well-used book of prayers out of His pocket – a set of prayers He has obviously used many times before. He selects one of these prayers, Psalm 104, and begins to read from it:

Praise the Lord, my Soul.
O Lord my God, how great You are.
Glory and beauty are Your clothing.
The light is a garment You wrap around You.
You spread out the skies like a tent
And build Your home on the waters above them.

Now begin to go over those words yourself in your own time. Think about the beauty in nature that surrounds you each day. Images of mountains or coastlands may come to you. The beauty of skies or ocean depths which remind you – if you allow them – of God's closeness.

Now listen to Jesus as He reminds you that He has indeed created the world around us for our delight but that the wonder that surrounds us is not enough – at least for Him. Without you it would be missing something. Try to grasp an inkling of this fact. Your presence in some way makes the whole picture complete.

*

EXERCISE THREE
A Fantasy about our Final End

Anthony de Mello sometimes asked people to think about their final end and he even devised a reflection that I make use of here. Most of us are somewhat reluctant to zone in on the conclusion of our lives but an exercise like the one below helps to sharpen and focus us and can also throw the wisdom or otherwise of our currant actions into new perspective.

First, go through a 'stilling' process. Turn your attention towards the final part of your life. Before that event happens, however, I ask you to take out a notebook and pen. The task you are about to undertake will be a gift to your family and friends. You are going to try and write a short account of your life. The first question to be faced is how you will go about the task.

Take your time and begin to map out the framework that will give your script some shape and cohesion. How will you title your chapters? You might start by thinking about objects in nature that you took real pleasure in. In your imagination, look around you and see weather patterns, plant and bird life, animals, along with the beauty of nature. Look at them. Smell them. Hear them. Touch them. For the ones that gave you greatest pleasure, give thanks.

Now recall experiences you have cherished. You want to describe them for your friends in your book but it may take you a little time to list them in your own mind and select the most treasured ones. At this point you may feel a little like a squirrel going around gathering nuts. You store the memories with thankfulness knowing that you will be able to find and dig them up again if the need arises.

After this, start to put shape on a chapter that describes ideas that have brought you liberation. In your mind, list off these ideas and try to remember where and from whom they came. Did the ideas come easily to you and even more importantly, how reluctant were you to accept them? While you're at it, cast your mind back to ideas and beliefs you have outgrown. Why do these beliefs no longer seem so important to you? Has their demise brought you liberation or anarchy – or maybe even a bit of both.

Next – the convictions you have lived by. If you had a motto that guided you in life, perhaps you might place that mantra as the heading of your next chapter. What exactly have you lived for? What has driven you forward?

The next chapter you may set out in your imagination will attempt to recall moments of risk in your life. What were those moments and how dangerous were they for you? Did the danger energise you or stifle you? You want your friends to know, so, in your imagination, jot down as full an answer as you can.

You might follow this up by opening up the next chapter on sufferings you have been through. Some will glory in this chapter. Do you? It may well be that you are reluctant to give any space at all to painful memories but if your friends are to receive an honest account of your life then your book must be one that includes warts and all. Therefore, try to illustrate what effects the sufferings had and whether they deepened, seasoned, or devastated you.

Next, let your mind go back over the lessons life has taught you. What were these lessons? Have you put the wisdom they offered you to any use?

When you are ready, move on to the influences that have shaped your life. Certain people, books, events and experiences will come to mind. Pray a prayer of thanks for these before moving on to the area of faith and belief in your life. What have you believed in? Have those beliefs – particularly the ones you picked up in childhood – matured and mellowed?

Move on to scripture texts that have meant something to you.

Which ones especially come to mind and why did they make such an impact?

You are coming towards the end of your book now and may have the necessary bravery and disposition to look at life's regrets. What do you regret about the way you have led your life? Are those regrets about actions you engaged in or those you omitted? Are there still unfulfilled desires that you yet may have time to achieve?

Finish on a positive note. Remember your accomplishments with pride and give thanks for the achievements of your life. Do this by thinking about what others will remember about you. End by just sitting for a few minutes, tuning in and becoming as sensitive as you can about what has gone on for you during the meditation. You have disengaged from the pressures and distractions of ordinary living for a little time and have taken stock of some important moments in your life. Try to absorb whatever wisdom may be offered to you and create a smooth transition period for yourself before returning to ordinary activities. You might bring the session to its conclusion by praying 'Glory be to the Father'.

BIBLIOGRAPHY

de Mello, SJ, Anthony, *Awareness*, New York: Doubleday, 1990.
– *Contact with God: Retreat Conferences*, India: Gujarat Sahitya Prakash, 1990.
– *One Minute Wisdom*, India: Gujarat Sahitya Prakash, 1985.
– *Sadhana: a Way to God*, India: Gujarat Sahitya Prakash, 1978.
– *Taking Flight*, New York: Doubleday, 1988.
– *The Heart of the Enlightened*, New York: Doubleday, 1989.
– *The Prayer of the Frog*, India: Gujarat Sahitya Prakash, 1988.
– *The Song of the Bird*, India: Gujarat Sahitya Prakash, 1987.
– *Walking on Water*, New York: Crossroad Publishing Company, 1998.
– *The Way to Love*, New York: Doubleday, 1991.

Anderton, Bill, *Meditation*, London: Piatkus, 1999.
Callanan, SJ, John, *The Spirit of Tony de Mello*, Cork: Mercier Press, 1993.
Cassidy, Sheila, *Good Friday People*, London: Darton, Longman & Todd, 1991.
Chapman, OK, Don John, *The Spiritual Letters*, London: Sheed and Ward, 1938.
Conroy, RSM, Maureen, *Looking into the Well*, Chicago: Loyola University Press, 1995.
Cummins, OCD, Norbert, *Freedom to Rejoice*, London: Harper Collins, 1991.
Davis, Roy Eugene, *An Easy Guide to Meditation*, Cork: Mercier Press, 1991.
Dolan, SJ, James R., *Meditations for Life*, Syracuse: Scotsman Press, 1991.
Easwaran, Eknath, *Meditation*, California: Nilgiri Press, 1991.
Fontana, David, *The Elements of Meditation*, Dorset: Element Books Ltd, 1991.
– *The Meditators' Handbook*, Dorset: Element Books, 1992.
Fowke, Ruth, *Personality and Prayer*, Surrey: Eagle Publications, 1997.
Galache, SJ, Gabriel, *Praying Body and Soul: Methods and Practices of Anthony de Mello*, Dublin: Columba Press, 1996.
Gawain, Shakti, *Creative Visualisation*, New York: Bantam New Age Books, 1978.
Greer, Allica, *Meditation is Powerful*, Middlesex: Penguin Books, 2001.

Griffiths, Bede, *A New Vision of Reality*, London: William Collins, 1989.

Grogan SJ, Brian, *Finding God in All Things*, Dublin: Messenger Publications, 1996.

Hall, Doriel, *Healing with Meditation*, Dublin: Gill & Macmillan, 1996.

Hoodwin, Shepherd, *Meditations for Self-discovery*, New York: Summerjoy Press, 1995.

Hume, Cardinal Basil, *Basil in Blunderland*, London: Darton, Longman & Todd, 1997.

Kabat-Zinn, Jon, *Mindfulness Meditation for Everyday*, London: Piatkus, 1994.

– *Wherever You Go, There You Are*, New York: Hyperion, 1994.

Kamalashila, *Meditation*, Birmingham: Windhorse Publications, 1992.

Mariana, Paul, *Thirty Days on Retreat with the Exercises of St Ignatius*, New York: Viking Compass Press, 2003.

McRae, David & Frenkel, Dean, *The Essential Meditation Guide*, Melbourne: Hill of Content Publishing, 1994.

Merton, Thomas, *The Wisdom of the Desert*, New York: New Directions Publications, 1960.

Monahan, Luke (ed.), *Suicide, Bereavement and Loss*, Dublin: Irish Association of Pastoral Care in Education, 1999.

Moore, Thomas, *Meditations*, New York: Harper Collins, 1994.

Mother Mary Clare SLG, *Learning to Pray*, Oxford: Convent of the Incarnation, 1970.

Naranjo, Claudio and Ornstein, Robert, *The Psychology of Meditation*, New York: Viking Press, 1971.

Ozaniel, Naomi, *Meditation in a Week*, London: Hodder & Stoughton, 1993.

Pennington, OCSO, M. Basil, *Centering Prayer*, New York: Doubleday, 1982.

Pritz, Alan L., *Pocket Guide to Meditation*, California: Crossing Press, 1997.

Progoff, Ira, *The Well and the Cathedral*, New York: Dialogue House Library, 1992.

Reehorst, BVM, Jane, *Guided Meditations for Children*, Iowa: Wm. C. Brown, 1986.

Sanford, John A., *Dreams*, San Francisco: Harper, 1968.

Sindkins, Drs C. Alexander and Annellen, *Simple Zen*, Dublin: New Leaf, 1999.

Studies in the Spirituality of Jesuits, Issue on Jesuits Praying, November 1989.

Walsch, Neale Donald, *Conversations with God*, Charlottesville: Hampton Roads Publishing, 1997.

Walters, J. Donald, *Meditation for Starters*, California: Crystal Clarity, 1996.

THERE ARE THREE VIDEOS BY FR ANTHONY DE MELLO, SJ, AVAILABLE:

– *Wake Up: Spirituality for Today with Tony de Mello*, SJ, Tabor Publishing.

– *A Way to God for Today*, Tabor Publishing.

– *Rediscovery of Life*, Veritas, Dublin.

SOME USEFUL TAPES WHICH CAN BE USED AS BACKGROUND FOR MEDITATION:

AquaMarine, Stairway, England: New World Cassettes, 1987.

Byrne, Seamus, *The Healer*, Wicklow: New Life Music, SOL Productions Ltd, 1992.

Chapman, Philip, *Celestial Guardian*, England: New World Cassettes, 1990.

– *Return of the Angels*, England: New World Cassettes.

Haas, David, *As Water to the Thirsty*, USA: GIA Publications Inc., 1987.

Hudson, David, *Guardians of the Reef*, Australia: Indigenous Australia.

Hughes, Anton Charles, *Whirling Waters*, London: Hallmark, 1995.

Just Waves and Gulls, Wicklow: New Life Music, SOL Productions Ltd, 1993.

Miles, Anthony, *Even Wolves Dream*, England: New World Cassettes, 1993.

Oldfield, Terry, *Reverence*, England: New World Cassettes, 1987.

Spotted Eagle, Douglas, *Sacred Feelings*, USA: The Soar Corporation.

Wiese, Klaus, *Tibetan Bells*, England: The Silverdale Centre.